Edited by
Herbert Dreiseitl
Dieter Grau

new
waterscapes

Planning,
Building
and Designing
with Water

Birkhäuser – Publishers for Architecture
Basel · Berlin · Boston

Project texts: Stefan Leppert
Translation into English: Michael Robinson
Graphic design: Michael Kimmerle
Translation and revision of
14 new project texts: Jessica Read
Cover design of revised edition: Alexandra Zöller

Expanded and revised edition of the publication
by Herbert Dreiseitl, Dieter Grau, Karl H.C. Ludwig
(eds.), *Waterscapes: Planning, Building
and Designing with Water*, Birkhäuser, 2001.

This book is also available in a German
language edition.
(ISBN 13: 978-3-7643-7476-1;
ISBN 10: 3-7643-7476-4)

A CIP catalogue record for this book is available from
the Library of Congress, Washington D.C., USA

Bibliographic information published by
Die Deutsche Bibliothek
Die Deutsche Bibliothek lists this publication
in the Deutsche Nationalbibliografie; detailed
bibliographic data is available in the internet at
http://dnb.ddb.de.

© 2005 Birkhäuser – Publishers for Architecture,
P.O. Box 133, CH-4010 Basel, Switzerland
Part of Springer Science+Business Media
Printed on acid-free paper produced from
chlorine-free pulp. TCF ∞

Printed in Germany
ISBN 13: 978-3-7643-7245-3
ISBN 10: 3-7643-7245-1

9 8 7 6 5 4 3 2 1
www.birkhauser.ch

Contents

'Take thought, when you are speaking of water, that you first recount your experiences, and only afterwards your reflections.'

This piece of advice comes from no less a source than Leonardo da Vinci. But which of us could say that we have experienced water sensually in all its dimensions, to say nothing of understanding it intellectually?

Experience is the starting-point for this book. Experiencing water in nature, and surprises derived from conducting experiments in a water studio, finally led to the water features placed between people and their surroundings that are shown here. Because they make a contribution to townscapes or landscapes we have called them 'waterscapes'. Twenty years ago, when I started working with water in public spaces in towns and on housing estates, my first projects were fountains designed for squares in towns and country communities. However satisfying this kind of experience may be for a sculptor, it left me with a feeling of unease. I was particularly dissatisfied with one very common idea: water as a decoration in the townscape, a pleasant toy for artists and architects, but a superfluous one sometimes – and this is said while all the essential water management in the town, like for example rainwater removal, drinking water provision and sewage disposal, is dealt with functionally, scarcely visibly and without any aesthetic sense as part of the engineers' domain.

So on the one hand we have water as a sporadic superficial embellishment for all and on the other hand functional municipal water management, accessible and comprehensible only to specialists. And public awareness of this topic seemed to me to be similarly split, whereas in future we should be increasingly concerned with being able to experience water and gain insights into how to handle it sustainably. Because without this insight, priorities in society and politics will be too weak to preserve this resource in sufficient quality and quantity, while it is of existential importance for evolution and for future generations.

This experience quickly led to ideas about linking water-art with more complex themes: new and more visible routes for rainwater to avoid floods, comprehensible re-use as service water or newly designed approaches for more natural sewage treatment. I am also interested in human-aesthetic and social aspects. This led to a deliberate qualitative change in ambient and urban sounds with images created by the sound of water, or to light presentations using water, down to the air-conditioning of rooms and, just as importantly for people, to adventure areas, water playgrounds, art installations and to workshops and projects aimed at citizen participation.

From the outset the key to our professional approach and to the studio concept was working in an interdisciplinary team. Over the years, we brought experts together who were keen to go beyond their own specialist training as architects, engineers or designers and get to know other people's ideas and subjects, and thus become overall artists in a team dea-

ling with water in all its aspects. Through our work we have jointly met major specialists who are now our friends, and some of them have made a central contribution to this book as authors. They have written in essay form and each of them presents a view that is entirely its own. Here the sum is greater than the parts, and also the result of interdisciplinary work.

This book is written against the background of practice, and hopes to speak in the spirit of the opening quotation. The numerous examples of our work together, which has now extended over 25 years, are intended to be the principal source for illustrating this idea; they are arranged in groups relating to the essays. We look back on all this experience and these working processes with great gratitude, but this is owed above all to the people who made this possible for us.

We would like to thank our authors and friends for their expert work and patience in co-ordinating the essays: Professor Wolfgang Geiger, Professor Detlev Ipsen, Wolfram Schwenk, Robert Woodward and not least my colleagues in the Dreiseitl studio.

We were able to secure the services of Stefan Leppert for the project texts and also for editorial work on the essays. We owe this rewarding co-operation a large number of stimulating ideas. Michael Kimmerle dealt with layout and graphics in a masterly fashion. Not least, we would like to thank our publisher, and here we are particularly grateful to Ria Stein, who has worked with us and advised us most attentively, and edited the text as a whole.

This book first came out in 2001 and sold out quickly. The great success of the first edition thus proved the topical relevance of the themes we deal with. This second, revised edition has given us the opportunity to include 14 new international projects. Many of the works from the first edition have been expanded or updated with new image material and some with more extensive texts. The essays of the first edition have lost nothing of their relevance to the present, and consequently have all been kept.

We hope that this second edition will also be a success, and that it will supply impetus for steps towards a healthy environment, a synergy which is most essential for our socio-cultural needs. Water calls for imaginative design.

Herbert Dreiseitl

Water in landscape

Robert Woodward

Water is not just a vital element in our lives, it can also be experienced in a whole variety of ways. It creates different kinds of atmosphere and moods that appeal to our feelings.

Water is a universal landscape element. It is the vital element which can bring life to any landscape; immediate life, constant life. Water's wonderful contribution to this world has been to shape the hard landscape through its immense forces of erosion and to create the soft landscape through its gentle nurture of vegetation.

In itself it is the fundamental soft element. It is a sculptural medium unsurpassed in its potential to make the most of its form, transparency, reflectivity, refractivity, colour, movement and sound. It is a most desirable medium for a landscape designer. But such bounty is not gratuitous. It demands knowledge and understanding for effective use.

Knowledge can be acquired through study, both theoretical and practical.

There is an abundance of theoretical knowledge available. Most of this is for industrial, civil or naval application and thus has little direct relevance to water as a landscape element. While it may be of little use in creative design, however, it is of utmost value in analysing how interesting water effects occur. Knowledge is necessary to be able to incorporate such water effects in design concepts and to sustain them in finished works.

Practical knowledge comes from experience acquired through observation, photography, sketches, written description and physical contact. The physics of ripples are demonstrated by the appearance and disappearance of fine silvery texture on the water surface which can be seen when a zephyr brushes a still lake. The forces inherent in the motion of large waves can be felt by swimmers. The circular pull up and down, and to and fro, can be felt by standing still in the swell of passing waves.

Understanding comes from knowledge, through thought and an open mind.

Fountains are usually created as a response to a design brief which includes the client's budget, time limitations, desired life, durability, maintenance availability, water supply and, especially, the chosen site. The site can be a rich complex of properties of space, scale, climate, existing environment, character and people's activities. These can be seen as constraints or can be thankfully accepted as opportunities by a creative designer. Knowledge and understanding of water and sensitive appreciation of its character are helpful with these projects.

Water can create an atmosphere which stirs almost any emotion.

In nature many factors contribute to the character of water:

Setting Consider a bronze bowl brimming with water. How it would seem on a dry dusty desert plain as compared with immersion in the lush green growth of a rainforest gully? It would conjure up quite different feelings. Think of the same bowl high on a rocky snow covered mountain, in a city surrounded by tall buildings or in a suburban garden.

Containment Effects vary with the containment of the water body. Open expansive freedom when edged by a gradually shelving sandy beach. Restriction between high rock walls in a river gorge. Scattered, hardly defined at all, almost lost among the reeds of a swamp. Globules of dew, shaped by surface tension, on a soft green leaf. Wetted surface of pavement, free of binding surface tension.

Movement Water is never more beautiful than when it is still. Motionless, a small pond or a vast ocean instils a sense of peace of mind. The tranquility of water is conveyed to anyone who cares to stop. Steady gravity flow in rivers and canals or currents from tides in the sea, cause surface undulations or swell. This gentle activation of the water surface conveys a related mood change in people. The feeling varies according to the water mass and velocity of the lazy-smooth or writhing-sensuous undulations.

The description 'blackwater' applies when the surface is unbroken, no matter how active or massive the movement. This is an apt term to be applied because the water itself can hardly be seen. When the surface is broken, air bubbles are taken in. These bubbles form a multitude of spheres which reflect light and so make the water much more visible, especially in depth. This is called 'whitewater': cascades, waterfalls, tzunamis.

Lighting In the dark, the presence of water may be sensed by sound or smell. Even when it cannot be seen, its presence is felt. It is not always necessary to light water. Sometimes the gentlest light from the moon accentuates mysticism. This is so when the smooth sensuous surface of oozing blackwater is highlighted by bright reflected images of the moon. This beauty owes a debt to the small, relatively intense light source. The effect of disbursed, low intensity, light from a dull winter sky on an exposed stretch of water may make people feel more depressed and even cold because that is how the water appears.

Man made water elements are often best lit by existing area lighting which makes them coherent with the environment. Sunlight is desirable when water action and excitement are to be maximized. The brilliance of sunlight shows as sparkle on reflective surfaces, illuminates each curvatious bubble and penetrates clear water to show pool bottoms or make moving wave shadows. A mixture of sun and shade gives complexity and introduces time to the equation by varying effects as the sun's position changes from sunrise to sunset. Lighting utilizes the optical qualities of water's transparency with reflection and refraction. Artificial lighting can create new expressions by free choice of light sources.

Wind Streams flow regularly unless loaded by heavy rain, tides follow a consistent pattern unless disturbed by major earth movement, but wind changes dramatically season by season, day by day or even moment by moment.

Motionless air at the surface leaves water completely smooth like a mirror. The gentlest air flow is usually light puffs which brush the surface and disturb patches of the mirror intermittently. Air does not flow at a constant speed at the earth's surface because friction against land or water causes turbulence, even at very low velocities. At more than a few kilometres per hour there is enough energy conveyed to create surface ripples. These are very small waves of up to ten centimetres wavelength which are called surface tension waves. They appear in an instant and can disappear just as quickly because the surface tension of the flat mirror can dominate and so kill them. Stronger winds blow up larger gravity waves. These are quite different in action as they have acquired enough energy from the wind to be able to continue for a long distance.

Gravity waves are rather like sound waves. They move in a constant direction until they gradually lose their energy, are impeded by an obstruction or are reflected from a solid surface. Reflected or refracted waves move back through primary waves and form interference patterns; absolutely fascinating and often beautiful. Constantly blowing wind increases the height and wavelength until monstrous waves, which can travel thousands of kilometres, develop. Winds are created by the earth's pressure gradients and temperature differential. Their turbulence is influenced by physical barriers. Wind blows water from jets and waterfalls to form spray.

Sound Sound is nature's most delightful way to herald the presence of water. The mellow rumble of the ocean, out of site beyond sand dunes or the gentle gurgle of a trout stream foretells what is ahead.

Water's sounds have all the characteristics of music, variety of volume and pitch, sharpness, softness, rhythm and, most importantly, harmony. Falling water in cascades is heard as a range of superimposed frequencies. The pitch and character of each sound depends on the mass of individual water units and landing surface. Massive bulk flow to almost weightless droplets fall a variety of distances and land in deep water, shallow water or even on bare rock and generate a multitude of sounds.

Raindrops produce different sounds on roof iron, sand or stone pavement. The level of sound from water can vary from absolute silence to a numbing volume.

Colour Water in nature is rarely a 'colourless liquid' as the dictionary says. Often water is tinged with vegetative stains or coloured with suspended clay. This clay being opaque particles, affects turbidity so much that a shadow cast on the surface can be as sharp as if it was cast on mud.

Most colour we see in water is either from surroundings reflected on the surface or underwater objects seen through its transparent body. The degree to which we see reflected colours depends on the angle of viewing due to the refraction angles between air and water (hence a fisherman's efforts to keep low and so remain unseen by his quarry) and light differential. A sunlit red and white building is easily reflected on the surface of a pool which has a dark bottom.

Depth 'The deep blue' The deeper the water the deeper its colour. A view of a coral atoll from the air is remarkable for the wonderful variation of tones in blues and greens in the surrounding seas. Light is absorbed as it passes through the transparent medium. Any colour from the light source, which is often the clear blue sky, gets deeper and deeper as the light intensity reduces with depth.

The joy of effectively working with water, by knowing and understanding the medium, is the reward for study and diligence. It is the same sort of joy that a blacksmith gets from forging cherry red iron and cabinet maker from paring sweet smelling rosewood.

Tanner Springs Park, Portland

Cities are expanding worldwide. Natural spaces such as forests, meadows and wetlands are being consumed and displaced. Quietly and permanently, an insatiable appetite for land is destroying the living spaces of sensitive wild animals and plants. In contrast, the recycling of abandoned industrial land for new mixed downtown uses is space effectively and ecologically used. The City of Portland, Oregon, chose to go down this ecological path with the regeneration of an old, industrial downtown city neighbourhood, the Pearl District.

Formerly a wetland, the Pearl District was bisected by Tanner Creek and sided by the broad Willamette River. Rail yards and industry first claimed and drained the land. Over the past 30 years, a new neighbourhood has progressively established itself – young, mixed, urban and dynamic, today the Pearl District is home to families and businesses. As the district expands into the last of the rail yards, the City of Portland engaged Atelier Dreiseitl to design a new park to bring green space into this previously industrial area.

Citizens presented their own ideas and opinions at several public workshops. Key design aspects were identified and developed during the workshops.

View towards the Art Wall. The inlaid glass pieces are an echo of the delicate grasses in the foreground.

The park seen from a neighbouring building. Property values have increased since construction.

The floating pontoon is the ideal setting for performances in the park.

The sustainable water concept entails the collection of rainwater from adjacent streets and other paved surfaces.

Overflow

Rainwater Pavilion

Collecting from Pedestrian Zone

Stormwater Cleansing

Collecting from Streets

With surgical artistry, the urban skin of one downtown block, 80 x 80 metres (200 by 200 feet) is peeled back. Time is reversed and the story of land development wound back to predevelopment days. The park is like a view port to the past. The long forgotten wetland habitat is restored to the full glory of its plants and animals. Little springs bubble up at the top of a large open grassy meadow, trickling down to a wetland pond, sunken 1.8 metres below street level. A floating pontoon crosses the water, literally swimming across its invisible and varying depths. Symbolic of the old city fabric, historic railroad tracks form a wave-wall along one side of the pond. Called the 'Art Wall', there is a harmonious contrast between the static strength of the rail tracks and the lithe and flowing movement of the wall as it oscillates in and out, the top also rising and falling. The verticality of the rail tracks is surprisingly filigree. The movement of the wall is doubled in the reflection in the water. Lawn terraces run down the two sides of the park, providing lots of lunch-time seating and vantage points to enjoy the park.

Children absorbed in play. The park was adopted by children straight from the start.

A spring trickles across the biotope, meandering into the water.

Oscillating historic railroad tracks form the Art Wall, a 'skin from the past'.

A planting succession from dry to wet follows the slope of the park down to the water.

Events at the official park opening were much enjoyed by the public.

Space for contemplation in the middle of a bustling city

Informal, paved paths lead into the park, creating flowing transitions, a design theme found throughout the park.

The swinging Art Wall, made from recycled railroad tracks, as seen from the Boardwalk.

The seating steps are a place for lingering, relaxing and chatting and give a formal frame to the wetland park.

In a special fusing technique using Portland glass, hand-painted insects are trapped in glass and inlaid between the old railroad tracks.

The Art Wall is 60 metres long and composed of 368 rails. 99 pieces of fused glass are inset with images of dragonflies, spiders, amphibians and insects, like animals captured in amber, creatures of times and habitats long gone. The images were hand-painted by artist Herbert Dreiseitl directly on Portland glass, which was then fused and melted to achieve the final effect.

The project was originally won by a competitive proposal together with GreenWorks PC, local Portland landscape architects. The shape and scope of the project was only achievable thanks to a consulting 'Steering Committee', composed of residents, owners, investors, businesses, city administrators and users. More than 300 citizens were involved in three public events where art, imaginative brainstorming and planning workshops informed and inspired the design process.

Tanner Springs Park is a space for contemplation. An authentic and artistic ecology, it is a place which celebrates flora and fauna. The park is an energy source for people. They come to enjoy its inherent and natural vitality, and restore within themselves a place for nature.

Inlaid glass panels glow in the morning light. Trapped insects recall the inhabitants of lost ancient wetlands.

A much appreciated space: the pontoon floats over the water below the Art Wall.

① Artwall – Typical Section
scale 1/2" = 1'

Town hall square, Hattersheim

Elevation of the steps and
the projected water cascade

The water pulsates its way gradually from step to step, falling into a specially cast outlet.

The individual elements are placed and assembled to the precise millimetre. Each stone is hand-crafted and produced individually.

On the route from A to B our attention is usually caught by the destination. The space in between becomes a side issue. In town planning the familiar phrase 'the route is the destination' became a platitude amidst all the enthusiasm for building and refurbishment. It was only in the mid-eighties that towns started to try to atone for their sins committed in the post-war period by transforming open space from being an area that had to be bridged into a space offering a whole range of different potential experiences.

This has been brought off successfully in Hattersheim. This little town has excellent transport links with various autobahns and local railways, and is close to the airport, and so has become a desirable and highly prosperous industrial location within the belt south of Frankfurt. But developments of this kind rarely turn out positively for the town's appearance – even though communities are increasingly aware that they compete with each other and have to offer their residents attractive urban spaces. Hattersheim found itself facing this challenge in the late eighties. The community focused its attention on the town centre and announced a competition for developing the area between the town hall and the municipal park. This was a marketplace, and they wanted it to develop a life of its own, forming a link between urban and rural elements: the town hall was intended to draw people, restaurants would be able to use attractive spaces in the open air, the route to the adjacent park would make people want to linger there, and also provide a new way of getting into the park itself. Water became the linking element in the Hattersheim marketplace. The steps leading to the town hall are the heart of the ensemble and the source of the water. An inviting or at least alluring gesture was successfully provided by a water cascade made up of flowform

The flowing water intertwines with the marketplace. Cafés and shops use the area as a foyer.

Towards the pond, the watercourse is planted and more natural in appearance.

The watercourse is an attractive element on the square and a playground for children.

basins. Herbert Dreiseitl had the basins cut to the millimetre from granite blocks, after developing and testing the movement of the water in his studio in clay and plaster models on a scale of 1:1. The slightest departure from the ideal form would mean that the water would not run as wished in its figure-of-eight pattern based on John Wilkes' flow principle, which is intended to be reminiscent of a human pulse.

From the lowest step, the water falls on to the granite paving of the market-place, runs under two five-metre squares and then reappears in brick basins. It then becomes a plaything, with a straight brick edge on the market place side and a curved one on the catering side, broken up with blocks of stone.

Here the water plunges under the paving again to re-emerge at the end of the pedestrian area in a planted pool. There it is cleaned and taken through an open ford into a pond on the edge of the park. It then runs underground to a tank, and is pumped back up to the source on the town hall steps. A way from the town hall to the park has become a way of taking people to water.

The stream runs through a purification biotope into the aerated retention pool.

The pond in the park is used for water retention.

Water remains visible and enters into a playful dialogue with the path at a crossing.

Purification biotope

Stepping stones

Watercourse   Open ford   Cistern   Pond

Longitudinal section through park watercourse

Water features in an hotel foyer near Neuchâtel

Spring water from the hillside trickles over a block of natural stone. It seeps through planted pools before flowing into the hotel foyer.

Here you can hear water – a musical fountain enlivens the foyer of an hotel in the Swiss Jura.

Cups are mounted off centre striking the long bronze rods as they are filled and tip over. This produces ground tones with harmonic series, and the bass notes are reinforced by resonating plates set on fine bearings.

The musical fountain with trickling water forms the central focus of the hotel complex foyer.

Water runs through metal channels and down to thin metal chains where it collects in small cups. These then tip over when they are full.

Water is scarce in karstic areas. And this is also the case in Montézillon, a small town above Neuchâtel in the Swiss Jura. This is where the L'Aubier hotel and restaurant and its adjacent farmland and sales outlet are to be found, with a panoramic view over central Switzerland as far as the Alps. The old auberge and the buildings in the courtyard were rebuilt from the foundations a few years ago and have been run on modern environmental technology ever since – this extends from solar hay drying and an integrated combined heat and power plant to using rainwater for all the toilets and washing and cleaning facilities.

The whole of the immediate vicinity was redesigned along with the buildings. A new garden in which the typical Jura landscape is presented on a small scale was created between the hotel-restaurant, which was brought up to date and extended by a new wing on one side, and the working farmstead with its more functionally designed buildings and land on the other. In addition to this, a new feature of this ensemble of landscape and buildings was water – which is a rarity in this karstic region, and thus seems all the more valuable.

The first step towards creating the water features is that drainage and spring water is collected on the upper part of the sloping site. It then gushes visibly out of a large block of natural stone whose surface has been polished to mirror smoothness. Following the meandering structure of the veins in the stone, which were sand-blasted and deepened for this purpose, the water trickles into geometrical pools containing aquatic plants. The pools are part of a staircase that is the main access point to the new foyer between the hotel and the restaurant. From here the water flows via an open channel in the paving and an opening in the glass wall (submerged wall) into the two-storey foyer. There it flows via two channels built into the floor covering of the main floor that lead to the foyer parapet and jut out beyond it a little. The lower level of the foyer is a good three metres below; the fall from this height via a sound-producing system in which the water becomes a musician in its own right is the creative climax of the watercourse.

To produce this effect, the water slips down fine chains and runs into cups that are suspended so that they can move; once they are full, they tip over. As they empty, cup and chain start to move like a pendulum and strike against twelve long bronze rods that stand freely in the space like a sculpture. Different rods are struck apparently at random. The hardened bronze rods, which are up to six metres long, start to vibrate, thus producing floating ground-notes across the full range of the harmonic series. Heavy metal sheets mounted on the floor so that they can vibrate reinforce the resonance of the deep notes and combine with the sound of the bubbling, dripping water to form sound patterns reminiscent of the music of the spheres. The water collects in a pool and slides from there via channels into another planted pool and then finally leaves the building again via a second submerged wall.

Numerous models were needed, as well as sketches, in the planning and construction phases of this water feature. The musical fountain alone called for a large number of experiments with water on a scale of 1:1; the composer Heiner Ruhland also helped with the tuning. But visitors and residents scarcely take any notice of that or of the many fiddly technical details: they are simply fascinated by the sound, the light effects and the originality of the whole feature, which extends over three storeys and constantly offers new aspects from different points of view.

Watercourse at Herne-Sodingen Academy

A fissure runs through the forecourt of the Mont Cenis Education Adademy. It suggests faults and subsidence caused by the mining here, and indeed, throughout the Ruhr region.

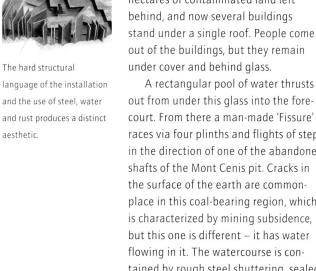

The hard structural language of the installation and the use of steel, water and rust produces a distinct aesthetic.

The Emscher Park International Building Exhibition was held between 1989 and 1999, in an area bounded by Kamen in the east and Duisburg in the west, Recklinghausen in the north and Essen in the south. It was also a ten-year celebration of structural change in Europe's largest industrialized area. This entire region in the heart of Germany was celebrated as an incomplete work of art that will in fact never be finished. Birches and poplars climb up the peaceful slag-heaps. Most of the pit-head gear has come to a standstill, and only a very few of the chimneys are still belching smoke. Printed circuit boards for computers are soldered here now, and scarcely any steel girders are welded. The acclaimed Emscher Park IBA ended on 1 October 1999. And the closing ceremony was held in a place that could not be more futuristic and that could not show the structural change to a service society more vividly: it was at the Education Academy in Herne-Sodingen of the Ministry for Home Affairs. Coal had been mined here from 1871 to 1978, and 30 hectares of contaminated land left behind, and now several buildings stand under a single roof. People come out of the buildings, but they remain under cover and behind glass.

A rectangular pool of water thrusts out from under this glass into the forecourt. From there a man-made 'Fissure' races via four plinths and flights of steps in the direction of one of the abandoned shafts of the Mont Cenis pit. Cracks in the surface of the earth are commonplace in this coal-bearing region, which is characterized by mining subsidence, but this one is different – it has water flowing in it. The watercourse is contained by rough steel shuttering, sealed with strips of plastic and concrete and covered with gravel. It turns several sharp corners, and opens up a little in some places. Triangular pieces of metal are welded to the bed on the steps,

The Academy interior: the use of water within the climate envelope creates a Mediterranean atmosphere.

Water cascades on the
terraces show interesting
flow phenomena, developed
in experiments in the workshop.

Plan showing the water
fissure and academy pools

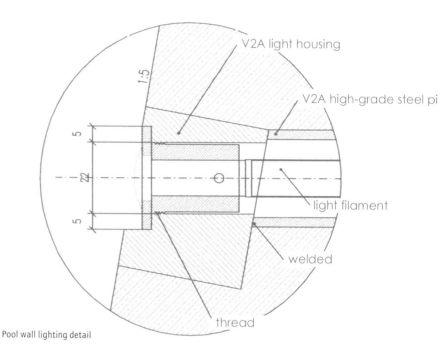

V2A light housing

V2A high-grade steel pi

light filament

welded

thread

1:5

5

22

5

Pool wall lighting detail

Section through a water
outlet

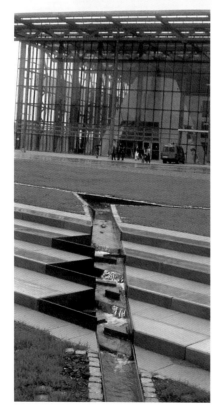

support plate (high-grade
steel)
cut for water outflow,
fixed with 'Halfen cast in
channels'
and neoprene

Abdeckplatte Beton
Fertigteil

300

70

40

WSP

120

100

cover plate, pre-cast concrete

mounting sheet

perforated plate, high-grade st
inflow for water distribution

inflow pipe, high-grade steel w
waterproofing steel disk in con

waterproof concrete B35

forming obstacles that produce interesting currents. The watercourse ends in the 'Depths', a triangular pool in which the water only seems to seep away. In fact 40 centimetres of water remain in it, and the water that flows in is pumped back from here to the pools in the Academy building. Herbert Dreiseitl sees these 'Depths' as a sculpture, rather than as a working pool of water. On one side visitors stand above the 'Depths', behind a barrier to prevent them falling made up of crude steel sheets 3 millimetres thick. The water falls one metre down from the channel into the pool under their feet. Opposite, rusty sheets of metal are placed on a metal plinth, arranged apparently randomly as steps. This is not a place for sitting down, but more a place for looking, for remembering the region's iron and steel days. Floodlights mounted under the sheets forming the steps plunge the 'Depths' into a mysterious light after dark. The 'Fissure' also makes a more powerful effect at night because it is lit. Water vapour emerges from illuminated chinks, an illusion to the underground mining activities that used to take place here.

As in numerous IBA projects, the 'Fissure' and the 'Depths' are intended to symbolize the transition from one epoch to another.

The water disappears down into the depths.

The water fissure under construction, showing the steel structure of the foundations. The Academy is in the background, with the largest solar roof in Europe.

A flow phenomenon detail at a slight change in level in the cascade – here the water starts to pulsate.

The new town square in Gummersbach

Plan and detail view of the sculpted installations.

Gummersbach is the chief town of its district, Oberberg, which it runs with creditable efficiency: the economy flourishes. The prosperity of this town of 50,000 inhabitants 50 kilometres east of Cologne has been on a solid basis from time immemorial. A small-scale, balanced mixture of industry, trade, agriculture and services has always produced – to express it positively – self-confident people. But this had unfortunate consequences for the central Lindenplatz in the 1960s. In an act of bold self-overestimation, examples of medieval timber-frames, classicism and Jugendstil were all pulled down and replaced with dreary progressive buildings completely surrounded by concrete slabs, everything grey on grey. And life gradually disappeared from the town centre. Now the town wants to get away from the dreary image conveyed by these buildings without any sense of scale, style or category, but they are not as easily pulled down as their predecessors. And so in the mid-1990s people concentrated all the more on the squares and walkways in the pedestrian area. And because a large number of individuals have an interest in these areas in particular, representatives from the local authority, the residents and the service and retail industries were invited to a discussion about new design ideas. The participants in the discussion quickly agreed on a modern water landscape. Symbolically this was seen to stand for movement, and possibly also change, uniqueness and something that was most convincing of all for the people of Gummersbach: a place where people would come to meet each other again. And they do.

One place that appeals, for example, is by the spring, with its fan-shaped, sculpted natural stone slabs, with lights between them to create mysterious areas of light and shade in the twilight. From there the water flows down a slight slope through a curved channel

Hands and feet can be used to touch and grasp water structures and currents – an experience for all the senses, and for the young and old.

Plan of the watercourse source: Water gushes forth from stone slabs set at different angles.

Carefully designed handling of waves and light transforms an ordinary object into sparkling jewels.

Idea sketch for the new Lindenplatz, a square in the town centre, formerly just a big car park.

The main entrance to the Sparkasse bank in Lindenplatz is accented by a 15 metres high light, glass and water sculpture. The horizontal, glowing lines of inlaid glass appear in vertical form here and blend into the space beyond the dimensions of the building.

towards Lindenplatz, guided by round prefabricated concrete units and running over cascades; on the way it disappears briefly underground, to provide a roadway for delivery traffic and rhythm to the running water. At the top of the square the water runs under an artistically punched-out covering into a jagged pool walled in natural stone. Long steps intended for people to sit on thrust out from the jagged pool into the square. In the pool the water flows over a surface that is designed with great variety, with little mounted bronze waves, for example, or shallow, curved cascades that create exciting patterns in the current. Floodlights plunge the water into a scene that is strange but made familiar by the medium of water, in which everything seems to have water flowing around it. At the end of this pool the water is taken back underground to its fan-shaped source.

The local savings bank is an immediate neighbour, and has taken up the water theme separately itself. A unique line of water made up of glowing, coloured inlaid glass and built into the floor covering links the wave pattern in the pool with a water-and-glass object in the façade extending over four storeys. As in the Nuremberg 'Prism' building, Herbert Dreiseitl commissioned the Dierig glass design workshop to melt several layers of colour into a flowing form, producing an unframed, self-supported sheet of glass. Water falls between two sheets of glass from a height of 4.5 metres into a planted pool of water in the entrance area, drawing in air from the outside through a slit as it does so, thus providing an air-conditioning effect. This gives the square its second landmark.

The inlaid glass is lit by fibre optics.

Particularly impressive at night, horizontal and vertical light structures are interpreted and reflected by moving water. It has become a popular attraction for people.

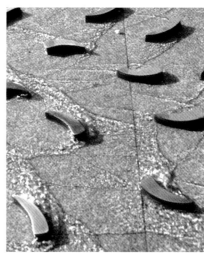

A fluid ribbon full of contrasts between hard and soft, crystalline and organic, running through Gummersbach town centre.

Integrated water design for ING Bank, Amsterdam

South of the historical city centre is the development zone 'Zuidas'. A new office tower designed by the architects Norman Foster and Partners is to be built.

A low cascade between the two towers and a soft wetland zone are highlights of this urban water surface, otherwise surrounded by buildings.

An ingenious rainwater management strategy incorporates detention and reuse of collected rainwater.

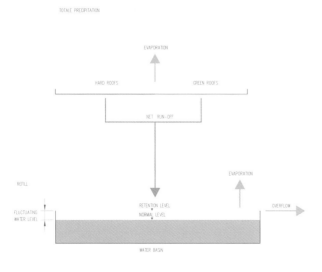

One can compare the flow of money to the flow of a river. The Dutch bank ING commissioned Foster and Partners to design their new administration building, named Vivaldi, in the new administration and services quarter 'Zuidas', on the southern outskirts of the historic city of Amsterdam. A blessing and a curse, Amsterdam has been confronted with realities of water since the city's very beginnings. Even in a booming business district, water is not just a symbol of dynamism, freshness and life, but a source of very real challenge for today and the future. Management and extension of the city's artificial ditch and dyke system is essential to control the ground water level and stabilize building foundations.

ING envisioned their new building being cutting edge in every sense, including water management. The City Planning Department supported this vision, delighted to be able to use the project as a high profile pilot example of sustainable urban stormwater management and a trend-setter for the entire Zuidas district. Between the two 100 metre towers a water basin is artificially constructed above the underground garage and sides the main entrance. The water features are scheduled for completion in 2006. Extensive and mostly intensive green roofs slow the run-off rate of rainwater and act as a pre-filter before it drains into the basin. The water level of the basin may vary as much as 10 centimetres, a buffer retention volume before excess run-off is slowly released into the adjacent 'Spoorlagsloot' canal.

The water body is aesthetically a very important part of the building. The very modern and minimalist architecture of the building is echoed in the reduced and refined edge detailing of the basin. The centre of the two high-rise towers is a transparent circulation well. At ground level, a terrace of water steps creates a social space on the building side and extends into the basin. The subtle waves created by the minimal height differences of the water steps softly resonate outwards, expressed by lines of underwater bubble jets.

Computer flow simulations and wind studies were used to best determine the locations of a natural plant cleansing biotope and surface filter to ensure effective cleansing of the water. A water storage cistern is located in the garage and supplies extra stormwater storage to supplement the water basin when water levels drop during periods of low precipitation. Through retention and evaporation, the water system is able to achieve an 80 % annual reduction of stormwater run-off. The trend has been set for Zuidas!

Open space for a residential development in Ittigen, Berne

Water dancing in air and sun

Plan showing central
fountain and overall
water concept

Revolutionary concepts for housing estates are a thing of the past. Outstanding examples of co-operative housing estate design, in which architecture and the planning of open space complemented each other in graceful moderation, are now listed monuments. Building firms operate on different premises from those of 100 years ago. But the desire for community, for contact between residents, is still the same as ever.

A bronze sculpture in the Berne 'Im Park' estate is an impressive confirmation of this. It stands at the centre of a paved circle in a round pool 25 metres in diameter, and points up to the light with three columns about five metres high. Water streams and patters playfully over the curved collar from one column to the next, then falls into the pool. When the wind makes the curtains of water into thin veils, the static columns seem to become figures dancing with each other – an image of community.

As in numerous other housing estates, open space plays a key role in the Ittigen residential park in Berne. Here 700 people go in and out of 222 flats in 12 buildings. They are looking for places where they can get together or play, for points that they can identify in the traffic-free inner courtyard, which covers about 6,000 square metres. The sloping site on the northern periphery of the Swiss capital offered an outstanding opportunity to put collected rainwater through its paces.

The water starts to flow from five source bowls at the highest point of the courtyard, then collects at first in a pool surmounted by large Norway maples. Large stepping stones in limestone from the nearby Bernese Alps accompany the water to this shady, highly authentic source point. Then the water flows down the slope, into gravelled channels. Occasionally a ford passes through these, made of natural stone columns placed

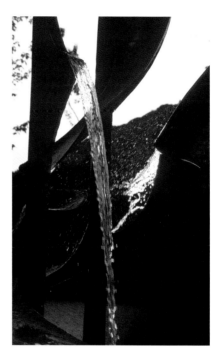

The central piazza of the
housing development
'Im Park' in Bern-Ittigen

Water currents – deflecting
and gliding slopes fascinate
children.

The water sculpture
in winter: the frozen
work of art plays with
the frosty light.

on their sides, and there are also concrete shapes that the water flows
through as gliding and deflecting slopes.
At the edge of the steps leading down
to the so-called arena, curved concrete
channels are built in, and the water
falls from these in a phased rhythm,
flowing on to the fountain sculpture in
a straight line and returning from there
to the source point. If there is a great
deal of rainfall, surplus water passes
from the fountain basin to two ponds
designed to be as close to nature as
possible.

The site has cellars under most of
the area, and gains its dynamic from a
thoughtfully linked network of paths, a
lively topography, from alternating open
spaces and intimate niches, and the
various opportunities to meet others
or to hide, to enjoy the sun or seek out
some shade. But without the subtle
effect of water in the pools, channels,
cascades or fountains the residents
would find it very difficult to identify
this courtyard as something special, as
their own particular habitat with lots
of intriguing sub-habitats. And it is not
until the water in the fountain sculpture
freezes into an icy artwork that the
three columns seem to stand together
properly for the first time, out there in
the freezing cold.

Who is crossing whom?
The water has the same
rights as the path, the
cracks allow for constant
eye contact with the water.

People walking at the
watercourse source.
The source feeds through
five flowforms.

Water is universal

Herbert Dreiseitl

Water is far from being just a designer's resource or a material: it begs to have its vital possibilities rediscovered. This starts at the beginning of the planning process for water projects, and involves linking up and integrating elemental themes. Knowledge of water's particular qualities as a material are needed, and often experiments need to be conducted to give a real idea of the result that will ensue.

Water is everywhere in our towns, in a labyrinthine system of concealed pipes. It is freely available, and can apparently be disposed of without difficulty. City-dwellers are usually only confronted with it at the various ends of the system in their houses or flats: coming out of the tap into the sink or washbasin, in the bath or under the shower, with the surge of the flush or when paying the water rates.

But nowadays it is rare to experience water in the open in our towns and cities – and yet it is increasingly in demand. Aesthetically presented and decoratively displayed, from a simple fountain to a showy water installation, it is appreciated as an invigorating element in front of and between the buildings.

Of course fountains and open waterways in towns and cities are nothing new. There is impressive evidence of them even from ancient times. They give us a sense of how closely urban design has always been linked with water and its use. This functional relationship can be traced from antiquity through the Middle Ages to modern times, and has made a lasting impact on the image of cities. Waterways for goods transport and other traffic, facilities for providing drinking water and removing sewage were crucial when choosing a location and helped to shape the ground plan of a town, the squares and streets. And here water was far more than something that simply had to be supplied and disposed of, it was presented artistically in all the great cultures, emphasized aesthetically and venerated. It created the atmosphere and expressed a living relationship between a town and its surrounding area. The way water is handled in towns shows more than the mere technical ingenuity of its citizens, it reflects myth and religion and shows the spiritual constitution of people living in a water culture.

This changed fundamentally during and after the industrial revolution: water and waterways were now increasingly brought under control. They were straightened, canalized, built over, buried and even filled in. Trusting entirely to the fact that all this would be technically possible. But this trust was broken by the floods, which came more and more frequently, and with increasing fury.

Now water is one of the key questions as far as the future of our world is concerned, as we have recognized that naturally available water supplies are finite, pollution is always just round the corner, and we are aware that water plays a complex role in the stability of eco-systems.

Water is the material basis of man's relationship with his environment, and often stands as a symbol of it. It creates links and is in a state of permanent exchange in relation to warmth, climate, air, soil and gravity. Growth, metabolic change and vital functions are inconceivable without water. Water projects are perhaps so topical because they express a profound longing for life in all its vigour.

Technology and aesthetics are usually kept neatly apart in our brave new urban world as contradictions that cannot be bridged. They often seem to be as far apart as the various professions and specialist disciplines associated with them – and so the various training courses are neatly separated as well.

Unknown water

Although we could not survive from day to day without water, we are usually aware of it only superficially and at particular moments. Reduction to simple functions like cleaning, washing and waste disposal reduces the intricate interplay of water with our lives to simplified and imprecise images.

Planning and working with water seem simple at first as well – but even the first practical experiences can reveal unexpected and unfathomable depths, and other surprises. For example, water often does not flow in the way that is projected by the computer or on the drawing-board: a curtain of water falls quite differently from the way you anticipated, the desired wave patterns do not materialize, or are not as planned, and the 'reflecting pool' you hoped for reflects too rarely – or not at all. And it is also not rare to find that the quality of the water in a newly installed system leaves something to be desired, or a deposit of limescale spoils the look of the expensive natural stone basin. Other consequences of such mistaken assessments and ignorance at the planning stage are technical problems and excessively high running costs.

This is not a horror story, but unfortunately it is often the case – and there are a lot of architects, planners, artists and their clients who could tell you a tale about it, and who have foundered on one of these rocks. They then give up, following the motto 'once is enough', or are simply satisfied with going back to banal solutions that have been used all too often in the past.

And there are some places where new fountains and water sculptures can seem out of place or unnatural. This is a sign of approaches that have been worked out in theory, but have nothing to do with the real qualities of water. Indeed there are times when people look at these fountains and sculptures and ask whether it wouldn't have been better to leave the water out altogether. Every artist and planner realizes when designing a water feature that water needs a great deal of respect when you are working with it: it is mysterious, and likes for be investigated sensitively. It is easy to assess when looking at projects and works of art involving water how thoroughly the people planning it understood water. Did the water in the project become a mere side issue, or is this a successful installation that does justice to water and brings out its best qualities? Here at the latest you see whether the planner had real insight, and how sensitively the water has been handled.

First experience and approaches

The knowledge we acquire at school and from the rest of our education is often not enough to grasp water in all the richness of its many manifestations. You cannot get to the bottom of water with abstractions like chemical and physical formulae, as the ideas associated with them are often too static and distanced. Water is full of dynamism, and it needs a sense of movement in the thinking and ideas of the people dealing with it. Professions that handle water every day gain experience of this kind and know the special inner flexibility that is needed to work with water successfully.

There are all sorts of ways of getting closer to this amazingly flexible material. This includes a number of sports that make it possible to experience water directly and physically, using some quite simple aids: swimming, surfing or diving, to name but three. Sensitive observation of water in a landscape is particularly valuable.

Water and air: You have to start by watching what happens when it rains. The weather front approaches trailing a curtain in the sky, and the threads of rain dance in the wind like a fine veil. If you are lucky, different coloured layers appear in the depths, and sunlight is split into its spectrum in a rainbow. Whether it is a veil of rain, or mist and cloud formations – the images change constantly, influenced by temperature, humidity, air pressure and temperature variations. But water is visible in air only when droplets or ice crystals catch the light.

Surfaces: If droplets fall into a lake from trees on the shore, you see a number of eccentrically expanding rings of waves, that seem to pass through each other without having any effect. Perhaps you can see from stalks, twigs and objects how the waves are diverted there, then break on the shore or are driven back again.

Wave structures with different patterns appear in all places where different media meet, e.g. on the borderline between water and air. Here dimension or scale has only a minor role to play. A fine breath of air, the slightest stimulus is enough to produce an infinite number of rhythmic patterns in a pool or the sea, or even in a little basin. Here again it is worth noticing the play of light, as it is only reflections of the sky, the landscape or of objects that make the wave structures visible to us.

There are planes that appear on borders, and also waves, that are only seldom perceptible. This also includes horizontal interfaces between bodies of water, for example with different densities. These are caused by differences in temperature or different salt contents. We are often aware of them when swimming or diving in summer, and they can oscillate slowly from time to time, as a result of wind, variations in atmospheric pressure etc.

Eddies: A twig blowing in the wind in a lake, stones sticking up out of a stream, the piers of a bridge in a river – the attentive observer will notice a series of eddies produced by all these obstacles. Whole strings of eddies are made visible on the surface by differently reflected light. But most of the eddies in water remain hidden. They are to be found in a large variety of unseen forms, in all waterways. It is not until traces of sand start drifting with the water, or colour is provided by clay or mica-schist, that all this diversity becomes visible.

Meanders: Even small watercourses, like melting glacier water, trails of water trickling over fields of sand below the tongue of a glacier in the mountains, shapes left behind by the falling tide on the beach or glacial valleys that have not been dammed show water's natural tendency to meander.

These examples could continue. A great deal can be observed in nature, but she does impose limits. Random factors caused by a whole range of parameters and conditions that are often unfavourable to precise observation limit perception. And therefore some questions can only be investigated by experiment:

Experimenting in order to understand water

Even though flow movement in water does follow certain laws, about which we know a great deal today, the specific ways in which they develop are full of surprises. Experiments can be very simple. The more minimal their construction the more astonishing the results often are.

A smooth, water-resistant sheet, as polished as possible, made of something like glass, perspex or wood coated with plastic, is placed in a diagonal position. Water flows on to the highest point of the sheet from a small diameter hose. You expect a thread of water to trickle down in an absolutely straight line, following the shortest possible route according to gravity. And this actually does occur at first. But after a very short time the thread of water changes its course: it starts to swing rhythmically to the right and left, producing a meandering trail of water that changes constantly. Rivulets, streams and rivers form these meanders, leave loops behind and reshape their banks. Entire landscapes are shaped in this way.

Different structures like pools, channels or vessels offer themselves for experiment. Flexible, changeable materials like clay or sand are particularly suitable for studies of this kind. If you wish to determine the inner movements of a body of water, you need to add fine particles or dye. To make surface currents visible you should add lycopodium (club-moss spores), and for three-dimensional movement in water the addition of magnesium dust or a dye like potassium permanganate is recommended. The closer the dye is to the same specific gravity as the liquid, the more clearly the movement can be seen, even when flowing slowly.

The water workshop: working with real models

It is sensible and advantageous when working out designs with water to work with it in a real form as well. Experience has taught us this: fountain projects, flow details or flow channels that are really interesting and appropriate to water cannot be developed and calculated theoretically, they need experiment, frequently on the scale of one to one.

We are constantly discovering that water is our best teacher. Despite all prior considerations and even with a great deal of experience: water does not always behave as expected. Corrections and constant new experiments are the principal task. The designs improve gradually and start to carry the signature of the water itself.

A water workshop can be simple and robust. In any case it should be well enough equipped to allow a large number of the desired experiments with water to be carried out. It is astonishing how directly and surely water itself holds the mirror up for the designer. In practice we are constantly surprised how immediately convincing ideas can be acquired in this way.

Linking themes

This is particularly true today: themes involving water are complex and are always directly related to other themes and specialist areas. Isolated water-features that are self-sufficient are no longer in vogue and on close consideration historical fountain complexes always existed in a context of many other functions. They provided drinking and utility water, were a sound instrument for the town, especially at night, and they formed a social focal point where people could meet.

Water themes today: the need for links. Water influences our sense of well-being in towns and in buildings, it affects the humidity, the temperature, the cleanness of the air, the climate. Water can be used in such a way that it filters, cools or warms the outside air and regulates humidity. Experience in the Prisma in Nuremberg or in the Nikolaus-Cusanus-Haus show new ways forward for air-conditioning.

Smell and taste make places unmistakable. It is one of the strongest impressions available if you recognize a town, a location, a season through its smell, and here too water can mediate. The somewhat sickly smell of the haze on a late summer's morning in Venice or the fragrance of blossom by the Seine in Paris in the spring.

The sounds of water against street noise. They are soothing, and compensate for urban stress, never mind the decibel levels. Robert Woodward opened his Opera Café near a busy highway, but surrounded it with a cascade of water, so that you can enjoy your cappuccino in the middle of it, undisturbed and in the best of spirits. And in downtown San Francisco you can escape from the noise of the city and lie down and relax on a lawn by the waterfalls of the Martin Luther King memorial fountain. But even unspectacular small water features can make spaces magical with their special sounds. In the foyer of L'Aubier, a Swiss mountain hotel, a stream of water activates a musical fountain. Water is the artist, the fountain is the musical instrument.

Moving light brings spaces to life. Water distorts, refracts and reflects. It distributes incident light dynamically in connection with its own movement. Working purposefully with light effects and thus using the water surface as an instrument is demonstrated by the examples of urban water in Potsdamer Platz in Berlin, by the finely differentiated waves and watercourses in Gummersbach or the major water scene in Hannoversch Münden. Here the art is to move the water in such a way that it supports the light installation.

Water at the wrong time and in the wrong place causes extra-high tides, floods, erosion and destruction, but also droughts, a lack of groundwater, dried-up aquifers and biotopes, and thus the destruction and elimination of a rich variety of flora and fauna. Water projects have to address creating a balance in water management. Retention, purification, evaporation and infiltration must of course be integral elements in a municipal water programme. Rain retention in the Kronsberg district of Hanover, the green roof to retain and purify rainwater on City Hall in Chicago and the use, storage and integration of water in the new Potsdamer Platz development in central Berlin all count towards this.

And finally, water creates atmosphere, something that is vital to our towns and cities if they are to be individual, unmistakable and easily recognized, with a sense of being home. This is a difficult set of phenomena to describe, and has something to do with the spiritual quality of a place, defining life and movement, which is something that water can convey directly like no other element. Interdisciplinary work and thought are needed to link themes together. The questions posed and the themes addressed go beyond the bounds of a single subject as far as the qualities of water are concerned, and this requires a new planning strategy.

Planning instruments and planning culture

Even since people have organized their surroundings, tilled fields, founded villages and settlements, they have had to make water into something they can use, and regulate water management. Thus water planning is one of the oldest driving forces in urban development, and gave rise to important engineering constructions at a very early stage in history. But these were always an expression of an attitude as well, of philosophy, myth and religion, they were presented aesthetically. Today it is scarcely possible to understand any longer how closely the fields of art, architecture and engineering were linked until the late Middle Ages: they formed a unit. An outstanding example of this kind of interdisciplinary work with water is an artist like Leonardo da Vinci.

In the course of history these fields have developed, become more specialized and moved apart. A real interplay of planning disciplines is rarely found, if at all. Architects like using choice sites near water, but it is exceptional for them to address other water themes and they usually see water as a hostile force that damages their buildings. Engineers are inclined to find purely technical solutions to questions about water, and often seem to be following a marked urge to convince others and themselves that those solutions are indispensable. Artists seldom make reference to this element that determines life and the environment. They often use water decoratively, as part of their own self-presentation system.

But water problems in town and in the countryside, which are increasing the world over – problems like surface and groundwater pollution, floods, drought and climatic change require holistic strategies and planning. Causes can often be found in the fact that such problems are linked with our social values and customs. Isolated repairs are of limited use only, in terms of both space and time. We are becoming increasingly aware of the necessity to work sustainably and far-sightedly with water. In the future planners will be increasingly required to put water itself back in a consistent context. This is the only appropriate way for dealing with its qualities and diversity. And here are some ideas for a start on integrated planning:

Global and local: Water always creates a relationship between detail and the whole. Each individual drop contributes to the balance of the earth's climate. Water projects become valuable when they help this process and can show that the place is being addressed, and how it is connected with the world around it.

Social significance: Water always stands for exchange and openness as well. It reflects fairness or injustice between human beings. Planning is successful if the cultural and social needs of the individual users are met and societies are regulated communally, and are expressed correctly.

Citizen involvement and participation: The way the most important substance for life on earth is handled is determined in many democratic countries by the priorities set by citizens. Water projects should include citizens and later users in planning and decision-making to as large an extent as possible.

Commitment and participation: It is important to promote and stimulate people's own creativity, as water is full of imagination, and a water-playground is one of the most popular places there are, and not just for children. Planning should offer people a chance to exert their influence and to suggest and agree to open possibilities for play.

Demonstrating sustainable environmental technologies: This means that processes for purifying and treating water, for avoiding floods and other such things should not be concealed, but wherever possible be presented openly and creatively. Retaining and managing rainwater in a new residential area can be integrated into open spaces within the planning process and become part of the architecture.

Admitting multi-functionality: This can be seen everywhere in nature. Why must a rainwater retention facility be used for this purpose only? Skilful planning means that play and sunbathing areas can be built in for when the weather is dry, as they won't be used for those purposes when it is raining anyway.

Integrated planning will always combine several water themes where possible. There are many of these, and they often do not exclude other types of use. But this can only succeed when everyone involved in the planning process really does use interdisciplinary working practices. Tolerance alone is nothing like sufficient here. The specialist disciplines should overlap in every individual involved, and every individual in a team should be aware of at least some elements of the others' specialist fields.

To do justice to water we have to go into the waterworld ourselves, experiment with it and learn to think in an integrated and interdisciplinary way about its flow and flexibility.

Visible water cleansing through a planted biotope does not just stabilize the water quality, but also adds a strikingly dune-like note to the austere urban landscape.

No parapet or railing – stepping stones lead over the expanse of urban water.

Large underground cisterns store rainwater from the roofs and make it available for re-use and supply of the water features.

Question after question cropped up on the top of the red Infobox in the middle of Potsdamer Platz, and deep abysses opened up in front of it. Colourful hard hats moved as though on invisible strings, and so did the lorries, full or empty after they had tipped their loads out, divers poured the cellar foundations into the groundwater at night, coloured piping ran to and fro over streets and excavations, cranes raised and lowered everything that was needed inside and outside, up there or down here. Expectations of the completed Potsdamer Platz were immense, and the problems on what was once Europe's largest building site were highly complicated. Two demands: people were not just supposed to work here, they were supposed to spend their leisure time here as well. A vibrant urban construct was to be created, which is difficult in the shadow of towering company headquarters. And the intention of setting high ecological standards for the project had caught on as well. There were the following problems: very little space was available for leisure provision, and it was subject to all sorts of demands and wishes. What devices for planning open space, what themes can be used to do justice to a lot of people and the urban design at the same time, and finally to come close to meeting ecological aims?

Herbert Dreiseitl had already worked on Potsdamer Platz immediately after the Wall came down, with an Anglo-German planning team. The theme of water as a defining element in the open space had convinced both the Senate and the investors from the outset. First of all the design possibilities caught their imagination, and secondly they were fired by the chance of meeting the ecological challenges. The suggestion that rainwater should be used for flushing toilets and watering green areas was met with interest. The same was true of the idea of using the rainwater that collected in the underground tanks to feed a water

Even when frozen over in winter, the water provides an interesting context for the architecture.

Everything comes together here: active life, prestigious architecture and a filigree pattern of water features that contain in fact just collected rainwater.

Canal

Rainwater management

Rainwater collection

Urban waterbody

Cistern

Overflow

Retention

Water use

Cistern

Cistern

Water storage in cisterns

Overall plan of the Potsdamer Platz site with urban water features

Flow simulation analysing how the water acts within the geometry of the pool. This made it possible to optimise the most effect locations for the inlet and outlet points.

system that would include a narrow pool on the northern side, one in the piazza, the large main area of water and the southern area of water. Additionally, this offered the opportunity not to lower the groundwater during the building phase and to make an intermediate collection of all the rainwater that fell on the buildings and slowly feed it into the Landwehrkanal. A complex computer simulation was used to predict that the Land- wehrkanal would only be compelled to absorb heavily increased amounts of precipitation three times in ten years; this is based on the approximate drainage figures for an unsealed plot.

To guarantee this, the system must carry sufficient buffer capacity. This is provided in the first place by five underground tanks with a total volume of 2,600 cubic metres, of which 900 cubic metres are left free in their turn for cases of heavy precipitation. In addition to this, the main area of water can still offer a reserve of 15 centimetres between the normal and the maximum water level, which provides a storage buffer of 1,300 cubic metres. A key feature was the water resources that were discovered above the turbidity level of the main area of water. Solids can start to settle in the underground tanks before the water flows out of source vessels on the banks of the south and main areas of water, through planted purifi-

Nutrient extraction through plant filters

Filtering substrate

Drainage layer

Impermeable seal

Circulation

Section detail through cleansing biotope

Sony Center

Potsdamer Platz

Philharmonie

A1

A2

A4

A3

Weinhaus Huth

Hyatt-Hotel A5

Büro B4

Nordgewässer

Piazza

Büro B5

Büro B6

D1
Spielbank

IMAX B7

Wohnen B8

D2
Theater

Wohnen B9

Staatsbibliothek

Debis
Hauptverwaltung

Volksbank C2

Hauptgewässer

Canarishaus

Südgewässer

C3

Landwehrkanal

49

Scharoun's Berlin Philharmonie is reflected in the crystal clear water.

Steps and sculpture platform in the mobile surface of the water

Architecture bathed in light, reflected and dissolved in the water

Turbulent rhythmic structures

The water surface is a mirror at night

cation biotopes, where it is cleaned biologically and chemically. If necessary, technical filters can also be used, which will remove any floating algae in the summer months.

In Marlene-Dietrich-Platz water flows in intricate patterns to the lowest point in the piazza. The water glides of flow-steps from the main expanse of water, and here rhythmic wave structures are formed. A detail that is accurate to a millimetre, worked out in 1:1 models. Then, immediately adjacent to the piazza, the water drifts from two sides over linear wave cascades, creating a clear link with the architecture. Finally water also emerges from a source in the northern area of water, then flows down a narrow channel. Given the extremely complex criteria that had to be met, DaimlerChrysler representative Karlheinz Bohn rightly pointed out after the opening that 'as well as the fascination that this idea exercised over all of us, it soon became clear that an artificial expanse of water creates a number of problems if energy-intensive technology and chemical additives are not used'. The results are convincing, as the quality of the water is good, the buffer capacity is adequate and the use of fresh water in the buildings has been reduced. In design terms, the 'Urban Water Feature' has given Potsdamer Platz a unique open space.

Stippled waves, created by the tiniest possible change in levels, alternate with smooth and turbulent areas. The interplay of wind, nature and art produces visual colour games.

The climate in the Nuremberg Prisma

The whole roof area of the complex feeds directly into a water cistern.

The glass building creates a pleasant atmosphere within the city centre. Waterwalls and luxuriant vegetation create a healthy atmosphere full of natural light.

When architect Frank Lloyd Wright built the famous 'Fallingwater' house in the hilly countryside of Pennsylvania he had one thing above all in mind: he wanted to blend the building into the landscape of woodland, river and rock. He produced a masterpiece that overwhelms visitors mainly because of the way the torrent rushing under the building is handled. Here water does not just help to balance the climate in the house. You can see it in brick-lined pools, on smooth rocks when it rages into the basins in the natural stone. And you can hear it when the shell of the building changes acts as a resonating chamber to change the constant rushing into the natural music of a region.

A lot is possible out there in the forests of America that could not be done within the confines of a city; at best it has to undergo a transformation to work there. But the architectural aim of blending the inside and the outside

Lush vegetation compliments Joachim Eble's sustainable architecture.

Using rainwater for natural air-conditioning, fire-fighting and plant watering

Air intake through waterfall

Exterior pond

Irrigation

Fire sprinkler system

Water-wall

Interior pond

Cistern

Rainwater concept with collection, storage, purification and infiltration

Rainwater

Cleansing biotope

Exterior pond

Interior pond

Cleansing biotope

Water filter

Collector pipes

Cistern

Overflow

Infiltration

Cleaning

Air intake through steel grate

Fan heater

Water spout

Adjustable wooded louvers

Coloured glass facing

Outer courtyard

Inside the glass building

Impact basin

Exterior vents supply the waterwalls with fresh air which is drawn down by the falling water, like in a natural waterfall, which is then filtered, moistened and blown out by the water into the interior at a wind speed of 3 m/sec. The system cools the building in the summer and heats it in the winter.

The greenhouse as a pleasant climate in the city centre. Water-walls and luxuriant vegetation create a healthy atmosphere and a flood of light.

applies in both places. In Nuremberg, for example, five waterfalls pout down at the same time into a set of residential and commercial premises that have been designed with a great deal of variety, using an entirely new design approach. In the 'Prisma' – 'Prism' – as the complex is called, removing boundaries was the key issue. Rainwater is of crucial importance here. All the water that falls on to the roofs flows through various cleaning phases into a tank with a capacity of just under 300 cubic metres, and is pumped from there into two circulating systems. Surplus water seeps into the ground under the underground car park. The first circulating system is used to supply the plants in the greenhouse, which extends over four storeys. South American vegetation grows in one section, Australian in the other, and both in a landscape of water-courses and ponds. These conservatories face south and south-west, and are part of the passive solar energy use concept.

High temperatures in the summer at least created a need for a second circulating system. Here the pump dispatches water to six water walls, which has a number of positive effects. Even if you have never visited Fallingwater you know how the sound affects you. You breathe more deeply than you have for a long time, each individual alveolus seems to come to life. The effect of the water-walls is like that of waterfalls because the hydro-physical processes are the same: the water pulls air down with it, creating a light wind. In Nuremberg, water falls between two walls each 5 metres high, which forces air out at the bottom. This stream of water pulls in air through a slit in the wall, cleans it and cools it – at least in summer. In winter the water, which is at a minimum of 18 degrees, warms up the cool outside air. This positive effect on air temperature and humidity is associated with a visual one. This air-conditioning system, based on readily understandable prem-

The natural light flooded climatising waterwalls are artistically designed.

Making the glass sheets: The colour design is achieved by layering fragments of coloured glass.

Layering glass fragments produces a three-dimensional effect after fusing, and creates interesting effects of light and shade.

ises, is presented as an art object. The walls are suspended without frames, and glow in fascinating colours, particularly at night. At the same time the structure of the coloured layers, which were fused together at 760 degrees, is constantly changed by the water as it flows down. The water successfully pulls the sophisticated and varied design of the space together – with a contained dynamic and by providing background sound.

Wind- and water-wheel in Owingen

The fact that rain is necessary but can be abominable often makes people feel that it never comes at precisely the right time. We feel similarly about wind, unless we are wanting to go sailing or fly a kite. Children usually see this differently. Wind and weather mean change to them. A lot of things emerge or start to move that weren't there before, or were standing still.

Herbert Dreiseitl wanted to make something positive of wet and stormy weather with his rainwater-wind device in Owingen, a small town in the hinterland of Lake Constance. The artwork has been at the extended primary and secondary school since the year 2000. As so often in his work, this object is based not just artistic, but also functional and even ecological. For technical or even financial reasons a decentralized, open rainwater concept was chosen, in which the lesser part of the water seeps away in a part of the building that is an attractive area in its own right.

The greater part seeps away outside in a system of hollows and trenches. But before the water turns the playing-field into a temporary pond, it sets a wind- and water-wheel installation in motion. Two wheels, each with two rotor blades and a water-wheel with six blue scoops turn when they are affected by wind or water from a roof area of 360 square metres. The three wheels are mounted on an axle with free bearings which in its turn is supported on an undulating concrete wall. At the highest point of the wall is a metal gutter that catches water from the roof and takes it to the scoops on the water-wheel from there its flows along an open gutter in the wall into a trench that in its turn takes the water under a path to the infiltration swale. But this undulating wall can only be a plaything to a certain extent. To protect the children from mechanical injuries from the wheels, a sheet of blue metal keeps the urge to climb within limits.

Water from the roof flows through a channel to a wind- and water-wheel, where it sets the wheels in motion.

The undulating wall with a rainwater channel is also suitable for play.

General plan of the drainage project for the new school wing. The majority of the water from the roof seeps into waiting layers of moraine gravel. Seepage pipes and basin and a trench under the building are used to retain the rainwater.

Infiltration within the building
$V = 4\ m^3$

200 m²

Green roof 100 m²

110 m²

Seepage pipe $V = 5\ m^3$

Pasture

Tiled roof
360 m³

Water-wheel

Undulating wall

Infiltration swale

Valuable rainwater is fed directly into the natural cycle via the wall into the wind and water artwork, via a wall gutter and infiltration swale into highly permeable layers of moraine gravel.

Administration Rainwater System Overview

Our societies are becoming more and more complex. But in the urban homogeneity and anonymity of the melting pot, is there space for true identity?

Queens is a New York City borough topped and tailed by New York's two busy airports, JFK and La Guardia. There are 142 officially registered spoken languages in the borough. Ethnic richness is readily visible in the bustling high street, a world market of faces, fruits and foods. Queens Botanical Garden is much beloved by local residents. It offers a quiet corner for morning Tai' Chi, beehives for a Russian bee keeper, facilities for a Korean flower exhibition and a romantic setting for an elaborate Hispanic wedding. Its general state of dilapidation was completely unreflective of its significance to local residents.

Queens Botanical Garden offers encounters not only with the plants of the world but also with its peoples. A public workshop invited residents, local businesses and users to get involved in the design process for the new park concept right from the start. Water was identified as a key theme which, through its essentialness for life, bonds people and cultures and the environmental reality of the Garden itself.

A master plan was developed taking into account new programming needs. The stormwater management plan is interactive, actively dealing with soil contamination management, new infrastructure, restoration of existing garden elements and siting of the new water gardens. These water gardens are thematically expressive of cultural identities and functionally active elements of the stormwater management system.

Funding for Phase 1 allowed for construction of a new green parking lot, and a new administration building. The green parking lot has contoured fingers of park which extend in from the Garden

and define the parking lanes. They are naturally planted and act as stormwater retention swales. A large area of meadow has a special soil substrate and under drainage to accommodate overflow parking for big events. The new administration building melts into a surrounding landscape of native North American plants. A green roof, and rain and grey water systems demonstrate quite conspicuously how principles of green building can be put into practice. The administration building and landscapes received a LEED Platinum rating, not least because of the advanced water concept.

The typical role of water for functions like cleaning, transport and waste disposal reduces the interplay of water in our lives to simplified and imprecise images. Sustainable water resource management combines aesthetic appeal and technological transparency while making a significant 'green' space contribution to our urban environments. At Queens Botanical Garden Atelier Dreiseitl went a logical step further by proposing a design that looks to express dynamic synergies between the environmental importance, cultural traditions and spiritual practices of water. Queens Botanical Garden contains ideas for a neighbourhood garden thinking on a global scale.

World cultures are an intrinsic part of New York City's borough Queens. Public workshops engaged local residents playfully and contributed to the overall park concept. Water experiments made participants more sensitive to design issues.

The water management concept is revolutionary for New York City and was a major aspect of the platinum LEED Certification of the project. Individual gardens are based on different cultural water themes and offer space for activity and relaxation. Water design and integration with the park were key design criteria for the new administration building.

Solar City Linz

Where the delta of the Traun feeds into the Danube, a new city has been built, lying close to a belt of sensitive wetland wood. This new city has optimal local public transport connections to Linz.

Overview plan of Solar City with the new bathing lake and the existing wetland wood

Resolving the conflict between city and nature is a major design theme of the master plan. Excellent and convenient play and relaxing spaces for the inhabitants help reduce pressure on the surrounding sensitive nature landscapes.

A lot of people would like to live and work in the same place, and this is also an accepted credo in urban development policy. It should be possible to realize life-plans for the population according to taste, in a graded system of upper, middle and lower centres in which both are possible without a great distance between them. But the queues of cars every morning show the mess that trying to meet these wishes on a regional basis has got us into.

This time-consuming and air-polluting scene is played out in the Upper Austrian town of Linz every day as well. For this reason the city of 200,000 inhabitants and a proud 180,000 jobs looked for somewhere to build new housing estates. But it was difficult to find suitable building land, as Linz is confined between the Danube and the Traun, with numerous protected areas. Finally a site in a typical landscape of water meadows was found, and architects of the calibre of Richard Rogers, Norman Foster and Thomas Herzog were persuaded to work for this project, which was Austria's largest urban development scheme at the time. The Dreiseitl studio won the competition for designing the landscape architecture.

The project was given the fine-sounding title Solar City Linz, and has raised enormous expectations. In the long term it is intended to provide a total of 25,000 people with homes in five centres. So far the concrete plans include one centre with about 32.5 hectares of building space for about 4,500 people, including about 20 hectares of open space. Doubts in terms of nature conservation are understandable. For this reason Linz's director of building, Franz Xaver Goldner, has assurances

Woodland

Swimming lake

Landscape park

Solar Park

Creativity room

Town centre

Schools

Aumühl Creek

In the green belt between Solar City and the new bathing lake, sculpted hills were built from excess excavation material from the housing construction.

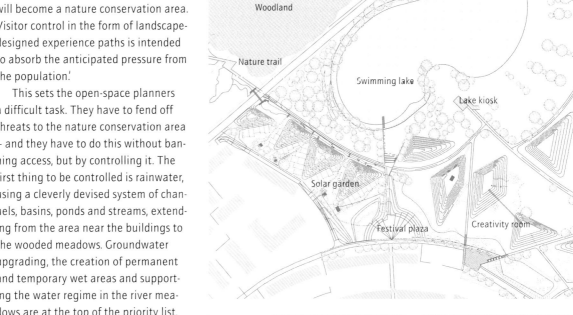

about demands and intentions: 'The adjacent Traun-Danube water meadows will become a nature conservation area. Visitor control in the form of landscape-designed experience paths is intended to absorb the anticipated pressure from the population.'

This sets the open-space planners a difficult task. They have to fend off threats to the nature conservation area – and they have to do this without banning access, but by controlling it. The first thing to be controlled is rainwater, using a cleverly devised system of channels, basins, ponds and streams, extending from the area near the buildings to the wooded meadows. Groundwater upgrading, the creation of permanent and temporary wet areas and supporting the water regime in the river meadows are at the top of the priority list.

Some of the hills are given particular emphasis as creative outdoor spaces. A water playground has one of these 'artificial' hills as its backdrop.

To protect the existing meadows from excessive visitor numbers, a range of different recreation areas were established: playgrounds, tenants' gardens and meeting places are in the immediate vicinity of the housing estate. Next to this is a park-like green corridor with room for a broad range of uses and then come the usual recreational facilities: a bathing lake, existing allotments and a new sports centre. The people who want to move on to the meadows are funnelled into walkways, given information at specially established stations and guided to specific places.

The unconventional design of the housing made it easy to incorporate collecting rainwater and conveying it across streets into a swale network.

A review of the results has shown that the newly created lakes, wetland areas and biotopes are being extremely well accepted by indigenous flora and fauna, even in areas directly adjacent to buildings. The new swimming lake is much loved by residents. The playgrounds, lawns and niche spaces are used by a whole range of different user groups. In a survey on living quality, the open space and connection to the nature reserve rank among the most appreciated aspects of the development.

Detail section of
the purification bed

The water is purified in the reed beds, which are bound into the overall design by a walkway.

The first zoo was established 4,000 years ago at the imperial court in China with a few exotic animals, followed 2,300 years ago by Alexandria and 420 years ago by Augsburg. Until the modern period, interesting mammals, above all bears, roamed in ramparts and fortification ditches, contained in special pits or enclosures. Zoos have been with us for some time as institutions – though its functions have changed. In the age of extinction the show-places of yesterday are changing into reserves for animals that are under threat. The WWF's koala bear identifies an enclosure as the last resort on every second information board. But the view through the fence is far from revealing the gratitude of gibbon, gnu or giraffe. And the visitor's expression is often similar to that of the sad koala bear, who can find little that is pleasurable in the change from a danger-filled existence to a life with full board and medical care.

Zoos have to change again, and offer more room to fewer animals. The zoo in Zurich, Switzerland, plays a leading part in this field on the world stage. Working on a master plan dating from 1993, this zoo wants to go over to keeping animals in way that is appropriate to the species, so that their basic needs in terms of landscape can be considered. And this twenty-year programme also tries to make a contribution to conserving resources: the Zurich animals' basic water needs in their habitat will be met with recycled rainwater. The Zurich planner Walter Vetsch is responsible for new landscape design and modifications, but Herbert Dreiseitl's studio has taken on the water technology. The bear enclosure was the first part of the project to be completed, in 1995, followed by the waterfowl area in summer 1997, and the sea-lion and ape areas are at the planning stage.

It is not just animals that live in water all the time, like sea-lions, for instance, that make heavy demands on

These waterfalls are part of the water cycle, and the purification beds reduce the proportion of fresh water needed dramatically.

Even though they are a long way from home – at least the water and the rest of their immediate surroundings should be right for the bears in Zurich zoo.

water resources, bears too need clean water. This need is met by collecting rainwater from the surrounding paths and green areas and storing it in underground tanks. These feed the circulating system in the bear enclosure. The water is pumped up to a rocky plateau, then runs down an impressive waterfall 6 metres high and 3 metres wide into the bear enclosure, then flows in a stream to two little lakes. It is a considerable challenge to use a comparatively simple technique to process surface and circulating water in a way that is aesthetically appealing and drinkable for the animals. Part of the cycle of 2,000 litres per minute trickles alternately through one of a total of three filter beds in a vertical direction, before being returned to the water cycle.

A skilfully camouflaged gap in the ground prevents the bears from getting to the filter beds, though visitors are allowed to do so. They can cross the pools on a wooden walkway and convince themselves that great efforts are being made to manage water in a way that is ecologically sound. The zoo in Zurich has found an impressive way towards a new zoo strategy – and others will follow.

Tower Plaza

Watercourse with
water gardens

Plaza

Cleansing biotope

Central Lake

Natural rocks

Wetland

Ring road

Green fingers

The plaza at the lake is a playful and central meeting point for the new town.

Thanks to a network of park systems, rainwater is conveyed in open green swales from the different housing estates to the central lake.

Collection stormwater

Circulation lake and watercourse

Overflow and release

Generally, when one thinks of Norway, an image of endless natural beauty and intrinsic healthiness comes to mind. And this is mostly the case in a country of natural water landscapes. However, when taking a closer look at cultural and urban centers such as Oslo, even in this land of natural bounties, the worldwide conflict between nature and modern civilization is present.

Once a pristine island in the Oslo Fjord, in the 1950s Fornebu became Oslo's main airport and transit point for flights throughout Norway. The typical glacial topography was shaved down with bulldozers and machinery to provide the wide flat open spaces needed for runways. Fragments of the original landscape persisted, scattered disconnectedly in unusable niches. In the 1990s it became apparent that, although close to the city centre, the airport no longer had the capacity to handle the increasing air traffic demand. Because of the spatial limits of the island, it was decided to build a new airport 100 kilometres north of Oslo, today's Gardemon Airport.

The surrounding city districts of Fornebu immediately saw the potential for an attractive housing and business development close to the city centre. This new suburb will also feature a central park for recreation, simultaneously the site for sustainable water management. Fortunately, there was an overall consensus that the development should be carried out in a sustainable and ecologically aware manner, giving the fragmented but authentic scatterings of original landscape special consideration. Subsequently, more than ten years were spent carrying out soil remediation measures to deal with the heavy pollution residues left by airport traffic.

In light of these pollution concerns, water and site water management were consistently crucial themes throughout several stages of open design competition. In 2004, Atelier Dreiseitl was selected to compliment Bjørbekk & Lindheim's spatial concept with a comprehensive water design.

Every drop of rain water which falls on the roughly 200 hectare site is collected, cleansed and re-used, infiltrated, or slowly released to the fjord. An artificial lake becomes the focus of the central park within the development. A water axis connects the former control tower to the lake, conveying stormwater from the surrounding roofs, streets, sidewalks and surfaces and evoking the gestures of travelers – their longing for a change of scene, for arrivals and departures – in artistic water interventions along the water axis. Nestled into the lake, a promenade, café and light-ice installations for the long arctic evenings are highlights connected by less formal seating and shoreline. The lake itself is a stormwater basin accommodating precipitation dependant on fluctuating water levels. Overflow water feeds the 'froglands', a species diverse wetland area, before slowly seeping into the Oslo fjord.

The collected rainwater is circulated through cleansing biotopes which through simple, green and transparent technology ensure excellent water quality. During major storm events, excess water can overflow to a wetland area where, after several cleansing phases, it flows into the sea.

The central park is above all a place for relaxation and enjoyment for residents. The park design is not inhibited by the fact that it also serves as an effective component of the comprehensive rainwater management system.

The magnificent historical Sonnenhausen estate was given a water garden for rainwater management and to purify waste water. It is part of the little park.

There are all sorts of stories and legends about Karl Ludwig Schweisfurth. By profession a business management graduate and master butcher, he took over his father's sausage business in Herten, built it up into a company with 5,000 employees and sold it to a food concern in 1985. He used the profit to set up the Schweisfurth Foundation, and since then he has run an estate in Glonn, about 40 kilometres south of Munich, where he has realized his dream of alternative agriculture. Schweisfurth always had an affinity with art – he used to share this with his colleagues, and now he shares it with his animals. This story is told about the Hermannsdorfer Landwerkstätten, which are part of his property: he once painted the I-ging sign on the wall of a cowshed, which apparently by chance enticed two cows out of a corner of the shed. They put their heads on one side, then raced out into the fields to fetch their grazing friends. All the cows looked at the painting together until one of their number licked it off.

Rainwater is collected from the roofs of the building and fed into the water cycle via sweeping channels and fords.

Land art objects as viewpoints above the water garden

Schweisfurth later had some more durable works of art set up on the site, plain stone columns for the Landwerkstätten, and striking wheels made of willow for the Sonnenhausen estate. The Sonnenhausen estate is next door to the Landwerkstätten, and has established itself as the seminar building for environmental education. The outdoor facilities were redesigned in 1989, largely on the basis of plans by the Dreiseitl studio.

In accordance with the aims of the foundation, all waste water is taken to planted purification tanks near the adjacent wood, then on to a stream after it has been cleaned. A large proportion of the rainwater flows into various ponds that determine the aesthetic of the open spaces and are also used to water the vegetables and flowers that are grown. When it rains, the water accumulates in the yard in paved channels leading to the pumped water cycle, which

Water running round a fireplace – elemental contrasts in the closest possible proximity

Pulsating water movements appear in the flowforms, aerating and activating the water that flows through them.

feeds a well dating from the twenties. A curved channel runs out of the yard of the living section, swings to the right through flowform pools, circles a paved fireplace and finally ends up in a semi-natural pond.

Thus seminar themes on sustainable methods can be tested outside the conference rooms against the example of water management.

The squares and pockets of public green are spaces for winding down and creative play for adults and children.

Because of the high housing density, there is little space for surface retention and infiltration of the site stormwater. Consequently, rainwater is collected in cisterns under the houses and re-used for washing, toilet flushing and garden watering.

Western Europe is starting to see a trend in property development, away from mass quantity and towards quality and environmentally responsible construction. This is not through altruism on the part of development companies, but rather recognition of a market demand. Arkadien Asperg is an urban village nestled within the congested conurbation of Stuttgart, and responds to this increasing demand for high quality, individual living space. Commissioned by the property developer Strenger, the architectural concept was conceived by Eble Architects. As a harmonious compliment to the warm and consciously Mediterranean architecture, Atelier Dreiseitl designed an ensemble of outdoor spaces which significantly contribute to a healthy and pleasant living environment and the overall sustainability of the development. The project has been such a success that Arkadien Asperg was awarded the 2003 German Real Estate Award for housing.

Within the spatially tight confines of 2 hectares, space was found for a central village plaza by locating parking in an underground garage. Through paving details and reduced traffic speeds, pedestrians are given right of way over cars. A fountain on the central square is like a fireside 'hearth', used by neighbours to meet there informally in the evenings and kids who hang out after school. The plaza itself is used for street parties and other village events.

A diversity of semi-public and private spaces harmonizes a wide variety of passive housing types. A stream meanders through semi-private community spaces. It has a natural bank, and at more public points play elements: a stainless steel weir and Archimedes Screw. The stream is fed with rainwater and is an enjoyable highlight of the extensive stormwater management system. Rainwater is also harvested from individual house roofs and collected in 14 decentralized cisterns. The water is recycled for irrigation, toilet flushing and washing machines. Other stormwater run-off is collected in surface drainage details which contour roads and sidewalks. The planted dry stone walls, use of natural stone, wooden structures and generous informal planting accompany the stormwater features throughout and are part of the vocabulary of green detailing which lends a 'garden city' flair to the housing estate.

A stream, accompanied by a small footpath, is a characteristic feature of the central green area.

Glass droplets – water droplets. Movement and stillness sparkle together in light.

The garden festival at Chaumont is known well beyond the boundaries of France. The daring innovation and design savoir-faire shown here over the last ten years has set the mark for all other garden festivals.

Themed each year, the director of the festival Jean Pigeat chose 'Chaos' for 2004. Herbert Dreiseitl was personally invited to participate, and as an artist and landscape architect, to conceive two gardens in response to this theme. Both gardens were also presented at the garden festival of 2005.

'Tohuwabohu' is a word from the Hebrew which describes a primordial, creative nothing-everythingness. It implies more than the contemporary definition of 'chaos' as confusion or disorder. 'Tohuwabohu' inspired the image of a raw, primeval earth crater, beaten and weathered by wind and rain, with the earth's first plants (horse-tails fern, Equisetum) sprouting from a life-giving mud sludge at the bottom.

A dark entrance corridor screens the garden interior from the outside. The visitor is momentarily immersed in darkness before stepping out onto a metal catwalk. Mist oozes up from the bottom and curls over the top edges of the crater. Suspended over the middle of the life-giving soup, the visitor is in a completely different world.

The second garden was titled 'Solid and liquid'. Bars of horizontal, blue glass are suspended one above another. Water quietly trickles down, droplets forming on the edges and dripping to the next glass bar. The bottom edge of each bar is cast so that the glass seems to drip like water. The border is blurred between where the solid glass stops and the liquid water begins. The whole sculpture has an irregular, chaotic and spontaneous feel. On closer inspection though, every drop of water follows the same path down the glass. The apparently hard glass is brought into a continuum of motion, the droplets

shining and sparkling in the light. The whole assembly is reflected in the water surface below, filling the otherwise empty space.

Through their polarities, glass and water have much in common.

Erosion and decay in the Tohuwabohu crater. Primordial vegetation takes hold.

Rainwater management in Coffee Creek, Indiana

Without their craving for new things, without their inventiveness we would probably still not drink Coca-Cola, not put on baseball caps, would still pay cash at the petrol station and write our books and articles on typewriters. Americans enjoy their extravagant lifestyle, but inevitably come up against barriers from time to time, and are thus constantly looking for ways round them.

For example, the United States has come perilously close to an abyss with its settlement policy. There seems to be no lack of land, and yet it is worth nothing without the resource of water, and this is now scarce in a number of places. And so a project developer in the state of Indiana laid the foundation stone for a model settlement that also set standards. It is strongly oriented towards pedestrians and cyclists, efficient energy use, healthy building materials and development density, and as well as all this it is highly committed to intelligent water management. The only water worth mentioning before building started is Coffee Creek, from which the area takes its name.

In 1996, Herbert Dreiseitl made contact with an American planning group, and three years later he joined the team of landscape architects and hydraulic engineers responsible for sections of the creative and hydraulic open air planning for Coffee Creek. The project makes additional heavy demands because it is close to a conservation area. A master plan fixed the main rainwater management requirements: precipitation water flows via trenches with slits to infiltration areas that are topographically staggered one behind the other. These are completely planted with prairie vegetation with roots systems that are highly water absorbent. The entire system is able to contain once-in-a-century crisis rainfall within the area and allow it to soak away.

Detention swale with
local prairie vegetation

Trenches channel the
water from streets
and parking areas.

An estate intended to provide 1,200 residential units can only be built in an ecologically acceptable way with a cleverly devised system for the water technology infrastructure. But this infrastructure will not be visible – in fact the water will appear in natural stream beds, in ponds that run into each other over massive cascades piled up from natural stone slabs, producing a charming open space.

This complex water management will enable typical woods and prairies areas to survive – also because the entire water situation of the area, which covers a total of 260 hectares, will remain unchanged.

Soakaway trenches
for rainwater

Pedestrian bridge
under construction

The new settlement at
Coffee Creek was given a
central park. Sustainable
rainwater management
was developed for the area
as a whole.

Wolfgang F. Geiger

Water is neither inexhaustible nor invulnerable. But the intensity with which it is used today tends to ignore these facts, as we increasingly exploit and pollute this gift of nature that is so essential for life. If we do not want to have to dig for our own water in future, we must think co-operatively, decentralize, and establish autonomous systems for water use at a local level.

There is no other natural resource on which mankind makes such heavy and complex demands as it does on water. Although it is not renewable in part, we neglect it far more than other resources – just remember how oil exploitation was co-ordinated internationally. In contrast with this, we treat water as though it were inexhaustible. Philosophy, science and technology have contributed to this mistaken assessment.

On the whole, people prefer and have always preferred to establish towns near water. It can then be exploited directly, it is a transport medium that promotes trade, and it contributes to the well-being of the inhabitants. Water in a town fulfils cultural, architectural and social functions. The urban hydrologist Murray McPherson was emphatically pushing for planning of the water economy to meet social and ecological requirements as early as 1970.

Water was comprehensively studied and managed even in ancient cites like Miletus. This requires creativity that can combine art and design, social perceptions, insights into handling water and technical innovation. It was probably this universal appeal that inspired so many scholars to occupy themselves with water. Thales of Miletus (624–545 BC) reflected on the water cycle, Plato (427–347 BC) later philosophized about it and Palissy (1510–1590) provided scientific justifications. Annually recurring precipitation or springs and rivers that never dry up give people the feeling that water is limit-lessly available – which is often reflected today in senseless use of water in precisely those cities where there is a drought. In recent times, despite all the insights and knowledge about it, water has become a utility whose origins we do not think about, that we simply use and throw away.

Towns have always been the heaviest water users. If local supplies were not sufficient, water was brought from near and far – according to the technology available. Thus the resource was exploited beyond the extent to which it could be renewed, and the natural water cycle was permanently damaged. The devastating effects of urban growth and user behaviour were simply not seen at first. Increasingly more efficient technologies opened up new supplies like deep groundwater, for example, that could not be regenerated. Large dams on rivers in arid areas, often the life-arteries for many different peoples,

may show the life-giving attributes of water, but they can also be a threat to peace. Low water charges, well below its market value, have also led to errors of judgement about the availability of water. Thus users remain unaware of the price they are really paying for water, and this leads to careless handling of the resource. For example, in an Indian community in which there was a major drought, water was brought in at great expense and distributed free of charge. This meant that users were not able to recognize the true value of water and left the taps running night and day even when no water was being used. This was justified by pointing out that the water did not cost anything.

There has been a failure to take precautions when dealing with water in the past. Problems arising from excessive consumption were often not recognized in time. And then when the problems were recognized they did not all generate appropriate pressure leading to political action, not all the solutions that were determined politically led to decisions that could be implemented, and those decisions did not all lead to concrete measures. Such measures were frequently consequence-driven, local case-by-case decisions that were made in response to damage, but not to causes. Here the 'enemy approach' was generally taken: excess or dirty water had to be removed from towns as quickly as possible. Measures were designed to meet a purpose, and not integrated into comprehensive planning appropriate to the complexity of the water cycle. Thus the groundwater level was inevitably lowered in many urban areas, flooding increased, and natural plant and animal habitats were destroyed.

The larger cities become, the more they seem to use water regardless of the consequences. For example, Peking is a city with millions of inhabitants. The groundwater level is going down annually by over 2 metres, but water is used for air conditioning plants, cleaning cars and street cleaning, huge sprinkler systems are installed for green areas and rainwater is removed from the city in large channels. A Mediterranean tourist uses a thousand litres of water a day, even though it is a particular scarce commodity in the region in the summer months. Water is wasted all over the world, in countries with rapidly growing cities that are in the early stages of industrialization, in industrialized countries growing at a moderate rate, in regions that have little water and regions that have a lot of water. At the same time there are already a billion people who do not have adequate supplies of drinking water, two billion people have no sanitary facilities and four billion people produce contaminated water that is not subsequently purified to a sufficient extent. Additionally, thoughtless introduction of harmful chemicals and bacteriologically polluted sewage into the ground and water often makes the water unusable unless it is expensively purified. Far too little attention is paid to the hidden chemical time bombs that are lying in wait in the ground and in sediments. These harmful materials could be reactivated by changed land use or climatic changes.

Thus present-day development of cities is often at the expense of future generations, and the gravest errors of urban history are repeated: the environment is massively damaged to achieve short-term economic advantage and growth, and the profit drawn from this helps to make good the grossest of the environmental damage. Many developing countries are starting to make the same ecological mistakes as the industrialized countries. Cities often grow in developing countries before a solid economic basis exists, and above all before the necessary infrastructure is in place. There are few cities with the resources and personnel to provide their rapidly growing population with clean water and sanitation. As the majority of people will be living in cities for the first time in a few years time (an estimated 60 % by 2025; the urban population will double between 2000 and 2025 in South America, Africa and South-East Asia), the water problem will become more acute.

Mega-cities like the one in the Pearl River Delta between Hong Kong and Guangzhou or Japan's Tokaido Corridor between Tokyo, Nagasaki and Asaka are considered to be a rela-tively new phenomenon: a number of individual cities have grown together to form regional urban landscapes. Traditional water supply and disposal techniques no longer work because of their sheer size.

All attempts to secure a social and ecological balance on the basis of traditional environment protection measures only increase the imbalance. This means that even greater problems will have to be faced in the future. Changing patterns of employment and social structure can rapidly lead to the decline of cities, to unemployment with all its social consequences and to an inability to cope with toxic industrial waste that has been improperly disposed of.

Even the responsible politicians are gradually realizing that economic development and the condition of the environment, including water availability, can no longer be treated separately. Irresponsible use of water as a resource limits growth and rapidly destroys what has been created. Thus poverty is at the same time both a principal cause and a principal effect of urban water problems.

As globalization proceeds, even today cities are caught up in world-wide economic competition. If sustainable economic development is to be secured, some rethinking is necessary: water requirements must be made dependent on the water that is available on the spot and in the immediate vicinity – water must not be brought in regardless of the environment and expense. A distinction has to be made between the elemental basic requirement, an additional social requirement and an economic requirement. We should remember the Roman system of water distribution, as it has survived in Nîmes. Here the supplies to public wells, commercial operations, baths and private houses were staggered so that water was obtainable in each case only when supplies were adequate. If water was short, only the basic public requirement was covered.

Water management can only be balanced if social and economic wishes are covered by the quantities of available and renewable water. We have to accept that urban water concepts cannot be based on prefabricated models, whether they are local or imported. Water problems must be solved specifically and within the immediate vicinity for every town, every district and even every neighbourhood. Something that works for a town can be inappropriate in a particular neighbourhood. Realizing this compels us to decentralize responsibility and action. There are many reasons for this. Large supply and disposal systems cost far more than small, autonomous systems. Small units are far less prone to faults. They bring small and middle-sized enterprises together to construct and maintain them, and thus reinforce socio-economic structures. Small, autonomous systems remain able to function because the people running and using them identify with their system and see it as their property. 'Water neighbourhoods' are also better able to take responsibility for preventive measures.

Decentralized water management fails only occasionally, but still does fail because of the structure of the water authorities. They are centrally organized and their responsibilities broken down independently: watering green areas, drinking water or sewage, for instance. As no distinction is made between different uses, this means high costs for water of uniform quality. As well as this, central systems are geared to peak requirements, because they have to cover end-user needs directly at every hour of the day and night. This too suggests a concept in which central water supplies meet a basic load and keep neighbourhood reservoirs full all the time, for example. This opens up new possibilities for reducing water losses, as narrower supply pipe widths can be used, meaning that cladding or smaller pipework can be introduced in existing supply systems.

So solving water problems in town requires a dual system. Technically speaking, local resources have to be used. Rainwater management is the key to the future. Water is part of a cycle in which it is used to water green areas and feed ponds that enhance the value of the immediate environment. Local people take the initiative in small-scale water-neighbourhoods. Public water supplies can then be reduced to covering a basic load, dependent on local climatic conditions. Economic responsibility is taken for a small area: the water neighbourhoods have to buy water in from central suppliers. In terms of water prices, a clear distinction has to be made between value, costs and tariffs. Here the real cost of supply and disposal has to be met by the user.

This system has a chance of success in the mega-cities because of the living conditions there: people live in a confined local environment, and spend their evenings and weekends in the immediate vicinity. They rely on local shopping facilities and leisure activities. Thus as a rule town-dwellers lead a life that is restricted to the locality, regardless of the size of their town. So the city of the future will have to be a city of neighbourhoods in which life-style and development are determined on a small scale. The central water authorities then follow the wholesale principle and sell to the neighbourhood units, who then manage their water internally.

The question remains of how long it will take to rethink in this way. Hesiod established the basic link between water pollution and the health of townspeople as early as 800 BC. At that time it took about three centuries for the Greek cities to introduce sanitary installation of the kind that already existed in the early cultures of Mesopotamia and on the Indus. We are faced with a learning process that will start in school and continue throughout our lifetimes. Whatever happens, this new way of dealing with water can only come from the inside, from the user.

Solving local problems by taking local measures does not exclude global action, especially as local water problems often have a lot in common. Hydrological and technical principles, the build-up of small water units and strategies for solutions that save expense and resources are transferable. Water-saving technologies can be used everywhere. Constantly rising demand, senseless use and mismanagement can be countered world-wide, by control through price. It is possible to lay down global requirements that all users are considered, river catchment areas are treated as hydrographic and economic units and that integrated overall water planning is set up to do this. The economic value of water is reflected in the price everywhere, and water users are involved in solving their problems, they can help to determine the course of events.

As eco-systems do not respect national boundaries, internationally agreed water management is essential. But within this global network the regulation systems must leave sufficient scope for regional and local implementation. It would be wrong to see globalization as doing everything in the same way. The basic principles must be recognized globally and implemented by regulation – then the appropriate solutions have to be found locally.

Global action should lead to solidarity in dealing with water. Here responsibility still lies with the industrialized countries. They are in a good position economically, and must therefore begin to implement the new thinking, particularly as they have dumped the cost of their growth on to nature and the environment in the past. Here making pretty declarations of intent about water protection is just as inadequate as suggesting to developing countries that they should handle their resources carefully. The development and environmental crises that the industrialized countries went through in the eighties have still not been fully overcome.

Global economic competition between cities must be transformed into global competition for the best ecological conditions, which will make cities economically competitive in the long term again.

It would be good in the year 2030 to be able to look back and say: in the last quarter of the 20th century pilot projects were started that created locally independent water concepts that secured people's basic water needs and also used local water resources following nature's model. And they also helped to maintain valuable eco-systems, at the same time offering people an environment that was worth living in, thus becoming a model for all new building and redevelopment models for the first decade of the 21st century. In many places, renewal went hand in hand with a change of thinking that no longer saw water as an everyday item to be used and then thrown away. Everyone recognised the true value of water. Globalization of markets and the media meant that these ideas spread quickly. The water problems that the 20th century had left behind were visibly alleviated.

In the second decade of the 21st century water neighbourhoods emerged in all towns and cities, and they took joint responsibility for designing and maintaining their immediate surroundings. Every household was geared towards economical and careful use of water. Municipal and regional privately funded institutions, linked with river catchment areas, were responsible for supplying the local water neighbourhoods and dealt with surplus water, preparing it for repeated use. A trade network was established between neighbourhoods, towns and the surrounding agricultural areas. Responsibility for water administration was completely separated from the supply and disposal infrastructure, which was geared to economic viability.

In the third decade of the 21st century, which has just ended, trade with water came to be taken for granted, with the price related to the true value of the water. State authorities retained only regulatory and controlling functions, and agreed these internationally and globally. The global network of main suppliers and locally based water neighbourhoods worked increasingly well. The neighbourhoods met emergencies within a restricted area to as large an extent as possible or increased the amount of water they drew from suppliers outside the region. Local people took full responsibility for their immediate area, and made this more worth-while to live in. New life was breathed into the water-related cultural heritage. Nature started to play a major part in the megacities again as a lung and open space, and as a shell for emotional and physical existence. The dual system had proved its worth and led to sustainable development appropriate to the needs of the present generation and not limiting the possibilities available to future generations.

This state of affairs was achieved as a result of perceptions and farsightedness at the turn of the 20th and 21st centuries. Thus today the whole world has become an urban network that is capable of acting rapidly on a local basis, and thus of surviving.

Rainwater retention on the Kronsberg in Hanover

We heard a great deal about the Kronsberg – before and after Expo 2000. But when the bulldozers have finally moved away, perhaps it will only be the local residents who find their way up this 43 metre hill. Which would be a pity. Whatever else happened, the Kronsberg development was one of the exhibits off the main World Fair site that was marketed and realized under the motto 'Man – Nature – Technology' as a model ecological project. As is well known, this challenge was not met in all fields.

One field in which it was successful, however, was the rainwater management in this new urban district of 130 hectares. The head of Hanover's environment department applied the word 'revolutionary' to this approach, which promised that the hydrological conditions would not deteriorate despite the sealing which the development made inevitable. The idea was that not a drop of rainwater that fell on roofs, roads and squares would be taken into the sewerage system, but would be retained on the Kronsberg or at its foot, soak away in part and feed a valuable body of water underneath, even in dry periods. This was largely achieved by two green areas, 13 by 30 metres, running parallel with the slope and various bands of parkland arranged one behind the other along the bottom of the slope. These three strips received all the surface water from the districts that could not soak away, evaporate or be retained in the private and semi-private areas, and in the district parks.

The retention and soakaway areas on the slope and at its foot are rightly called open spaces. Compulsory ecological measures are not seen as technical facilities here, but as parks. Water, even when it is intended to flow away slowly, or disappear by infiltration, and thus not a permanent feature, is an exciting and enhancing sight for all age groups in the green areas. In the two 'slope avenues'

The 'slope avenues' under construction; the stream is fitted with sheet seal.

Regulating devices are built into the retention lips. This means that the outflow can be varied and the retention frequency controlled.

Rainwater is stored temporarily in the sloping avenue open spaces and then runs down to the bottom of the slope in a little stream.

At the foot of the slope the retention basins hold back rainwater to slowly release it over time.

on the southern and northern peripheries of the development the planners made use of the slope of approximately 5 % with a cascade design. A naturally extended stream bed runs through the two green areas and takes the water to one of nine terraced basins, where it is retained until it soaks away. If there is very heavy rainfall the surplus water flows over the concrete retention lips, drawn on the site as civilization lines, and down into the next basin. The stream produced in this way is piped under intersecting roads, and footpaths run through the bed of the stream on reinforced fords. The water is intended to remain visible for longer in some basins which are an additional 30 centimetres lower and reinforced with a cohesive substrate. These are mainly in the areas along the foot of the slope and take up the water from the two sloping avenues and the surface water from the base road running parallel with the long side. A wooden regulating device set in the retention lip makes it possible to control the outflow quantity individually.

The Kronsberg definitely deserves a place as a show project in terms of rainwater management for a settlement of this size. It is worth a visit – perhaps especially after the World Fair.

Section through retention areas at the foot of the slope

Footpath   Retention lip   Retention basin   Railway line

Development of urban showing areas built by the year 2000. The sloping avenues and retention areas show up as linear strips of urban parkland.

85

The original barracks and
the topographical structure.

Topography and urban
structure of the area
as a whole

Even a one-in-100-year
storm event was handled
without problem.

Barracks architecture traditionally
has little in common with the quality
of life. The buildings are arranged and
developed from a purely functional
point of view, and people are not intended to feel particularly at home. And
at the time the people who commissioned them were scarcely concerned to
address the ecological consequences of
building. The Allied Forces have been
leaving Germany and going home for
years now. Quite frequently they leave
run-down military accommodation
behind, often extensive sites that had
little money spent on them and that are
usually more of an inherited problem
than a welcome gift.

But these sites also have their own
potential. They certainly take pressure
off the town to provide new building
land. But a new estate is only likely to
succeed if the planners are creative and
the barracks site meets modern requirements both inside and out. As in the
case in the Scharnhauser Park near
Ostfildern. This project involves 150
hectares, and is the largest urban development scheme in the Stuttgart area
in the early 21st century. The 2002
regional horticultural show is at the
heart of the site, and thus high on the
list of regional priorities. Horticultural
shows are increasingly inclined towards
innovative approaches to town planning, and so it was clear from the beginning of the planning process that rainwater would have to be treated in a
new way as well.

Two systems of streams flow below
the site, which is on a south-facing slope,
and the Scharnhauser Park surface
water is useful to these. The Körsch, for
example, often threatens to dry up in
summer. Additional water would sustain
the valuable biotope structure that is
the only network worth speaking of
in this region for sustaining flora and
fauna. On the other hand, to avoid
floods, the planners have settled for a
different strategy of discharge reduc-

The landscape steps are the
green backbone of the new
housing development.

RKB West

Höfelbach

Site plan showing
rain water management

RKB Ost

RKB Kreuzbrunnen

Slope

Krähenbach

Retention areas

Filter-swale system

Rainwater channelling

87

tion, discharge delay and modest infiltration into the clayey subsoil.

The rainwater has now been fully withdrawn from the former mixed water sewer and now flows, when it has not been retained in private storage tanks or in roof gardens, or has soaked away through water-permeable surfaces, through a system of channels and ditches running alongside the streets. This network runs through the new estate as an unmistakable design feature. Here the cascade-like landscape steps, 1.5 kilometres long, are particularly striking. This design element is also part of the rainwater management programme: below the steps the living bottom zone purifies the water in additional retention hollows and pools. Discharged water that has been delayed and purified in this way is fed via natural gradients into the surrounding landscape, with its valuable wetlands, biotopes and spring areas.

Even if traces of the former military structure show in the urban development, the water has successfully linked up with the surrounding landscape and its features.

Toppilansaari Park in Oulu

Tangentially staggered paths accompany the rainwater in swales on its way out to sea.

Connection plazas have clear wall elements which give the 'flowing park' an anchor and space for relaxation and play.

The park 'flows' over the street crossing and thus has priority.

Natural wetland

Connecting pathway

Ice Garden

Crossing

Activity area

Crossing

Water-wind-sound-garden

Few, apart from the Finnish, know where Oulu is. A town tucked away at the furthest reaches of the Baltic Sea, just 160 kilometres south of the polar circle, it is not the sleepy stop-over one might expect. World leaders in mobile telecommunications and advanced medical and electronic technology have chosen to base their businesses in Oulu. It is the city with the highest rate of economic growth in Finland and, consequently, there is high demand for attractive, affordable housing.

Toppilansaari, a half island between the canalised Oulu harbour entrance and the open sea, is the site of the Finnish Housing Expo 2005. The unique ecology and distinctive flora of the saline wetland on the sea side is made even more interesting through the proximity and contrast of the urban and industrial maritime canal.

The housing is laid out as a sustainable pilot project. A green park forms a central core for the relatively spread-out housing elements. The park provides convenient and informal recreation and activity areas which help reduce recreational impact on the sensitive wetland habitat. It is also a stormwater system, where rainwater and spring snowmelt are collected, cleaned and slowly released to the wetland via swales whose soft topography mirrors the flow of water. The proximity of the sea is further evoked by waved steel planting edges which are a repeated design element throughout the park.

'Toppilansaari' means 'Park of the Young Sailor' in Finnish. This name defined the programme of two land art installations which close the southern and northern ends of the park. In the southern garden, a conceptual, sunken boat is a memorial to all the young sailors who never returned to land. Masts are stringed like an instrument, low tones are heard from the benches integrated into the

Concrete stepping stones also function to hold back rain and melt water for detention.

Openings at street crossing convey the rain and melt water to the next park swale.

Run-off from adjacent roads and plazas is cleaned and brought to the 'flowing park'.

boat's 'hull'. A wooden ship deck frames a sand box and children's paddling pool.

In the northern garden, a light 'vortex' is an orientation landmark, visible like a lighthouse from far and wide. The light vortex rotates in the wind, variably lighting up sculptural surfaces. In winter, these surfaces are ice sculptures, which depending on temperature, wind and air humidity are iced up in bizarre and fantastic patterns. Both sculptures were consciously designed by Herbert Dreiseitl using recycled materials and constructed on site by local contractors.

The park accommodates a whole range of local and city pedestrian and bicycle circulation routes. At crossings, the paving is laid in waves, emphasizing that the park flows with a natural spatial logic across these intersections. The sites own unique and delicate natural habitats have been preserved and coexist with areas which celebrate the past and present history of the people who live and visit there.

Steel bands, part of a sunken ship, hum in the wind and remind of the young mariners who never returned from the sea.

Recycled steel sheeting, a wind-powered rotating light and mist are the key elements of the 'light vortex'.

Abstract fragments of a sunken ship are a space sculpture in the park.

Decentralized purification plants are particularly suitable for remote farms and hamlets in country areas.

'O'er seven stones the water flows, 'tis pure again, the farmer knows.' This piece of agricultural wisdom may well no longer apply to the present day and the highly complex ways in which water is now polluted, but there is a grain of truth in it: water is able to purify itself. Nothing has changed here. But cities have long since had to say goodbye to giving sewage the time and space to purify itself. They have ultimately arrived at narrow-mesh sewerage networks and treatment plants, via the intermediate stage of evil-smelling sewage farms. This is a hygienic but very expensive method of getting rid of the daily quota of faeces.

Fitting the sheet seal in a purification bed. Here laymen can help as well – a school class at work.

Since the early 1990s, country people have increasingly started to remember decentralized sewage treatment. An increasing number of farmers, but also private householders who have enough land, are letting their sewage flow not over seven stones, but through settling tanks and purification beds, so that it can then pass into an effluent tank having been cleaned. This also applies to the Hofgemeinschaft in Wörme, an organic farm in Handeloh, south of Hamburg. The Dreiseitl studio planned a sewage treatment plant for about 30 people who live there plus holiday visitors and participants in educational projects.

Setting the manholes and introducing the filter substrate

The planners took advantage of the natural slope on the site, and were thus able to do without technical units to a large extent. Thus sewage from the farm first flows into a 250 metre long collector tank and then into three shafts. Here a filter sack separates solid and liquid components. Alternate use of the shafts means that the contents of the filled bags can be pre-composted and used in fields and gardens after nine to fifteen months.

The decentralized treatment plant with purification beds treats all the sewage from the hamlet of Unterbach, which has 80 inhabitants.

Installing the substrate for a purification bed layer by layer

The liquid part then flows into purification beds with an area of 7 square metres per resident equivalent. The botanical treatment plant is de-

Planting the beds with aquatic plants (phragmitis)

Residents can service the plant themselves, as it is easy to manage; this gives people long-term responsibility for their own sewage disposal.

Sewage treatment for an agricultural establishment with nursery

signed for a maximum of 100 resident equivalents. The sewage runs through the beds in two stages: first of all through four 80 centimetre deep beds arranged in parallel, with a infiltration length of 5 metres. In the second stage the beds are 1 metre deep with a infiltration length of 7 metres. The plants that grow there introduce considerable quantities of oxygen into the earth- or water-bearing layer. Aerobic decomposition processes are then set in train. After passing the sampling shaft the purified sewage runs into the little river Seeve via a semi-natural channel with plants growing in it. Very little care and maintenance has proved to be necessary. The purification beds have simply to be kept free of undesirable vegetation and woody plants. The pipes and gutters have to be flushed out three to four times a year to test and maintain their ability to function.

The plant has been working without problems, economically and without complaint since 1994. The Wörme farm's treatment plant has thus contributed to regional water quality, but also considerably reinforced its image as an organic farm and seminar venue.

The sewage seeps through several planted tanks and harmful substances are removed by organic decomposition processes at the various purification stages.

Section through the various purification stages: sewage flows horizontally through plant filters.

Mechanical purification stage   Distribution manhole 1   Biological purification, stage 1

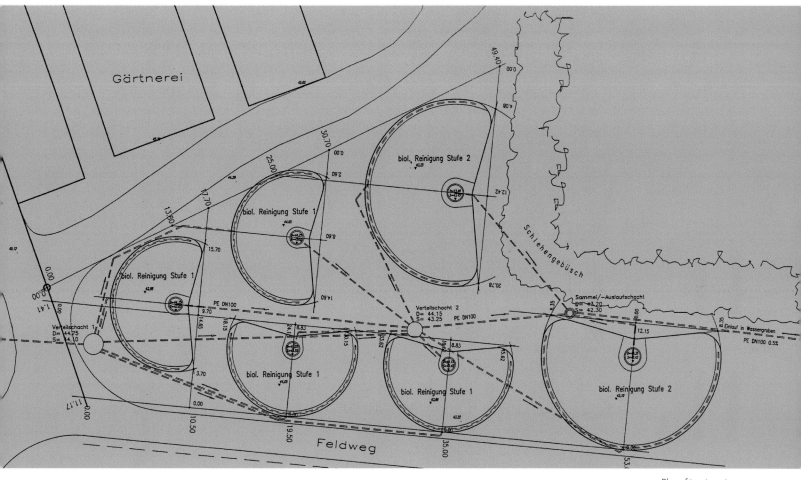

Plan of treatment
plant with various
purification beds

Distribution manhole 2   Biological purification, stage 2   Collection/outlet manhole   Drainage trench

The Volme inside the town of Hagen was constrained within a box profile with embankment walls 3 metres high. As the concrete bed slowly crumbled away, a complete change of direction was envisioned.

There are some towns that have a considerable number of inhabitants and whose names are familiar, but do not trigger any associations. For example, you've heard of Hagen, but it's unlikely that you can describe more than the platform on the ICE train line. It's the same with rivers. The Ennepe is familiar enough, but how many people know that it flows into the Volme, which is a tributary of the Ruhr? Only people who live in Hagen, you might think. Anyway, the rivers come together just outside the town gates, and the Volme runs through the town centre.

But in the case of Hagen's inhabitants you can't even be certain about the Volme. As in many other places, this town with 200,000 inhabitants at the southern gateway of the Ruhr has treated its river somewhat shabbily. It was downgraded to a canal in the past 100 years, polluted with industrial waste and hidden away behind factory halls. The municipal backyards are all on the Volme. For this reason the town brought its angry citizens into the equation when it was choosing a site for its new town hall on the Volme. The people voted to dump these plans in a local referendum – until they heard in autumn 2000 about the idea of making the river and above all its banks attractive to the population at this point. At the same time the open-space planners wanted to lay the foundation stones for a waterway redevelopment that was to be continued in the long term. For example, the bottoms of the waterways were to be roughened, two weirs were to be removed or at least lowered, and banks arranged to impede the water or to allow it to flow.

Hydraulic assessment of the previous state of the Volme and projected effects of a new design

Since restoration, the river Volme has regained the diversity of its river structure. Natural shorelines alternate with urban ones. Stepped terraces in front of the Town Hall restore river access to the citizens.

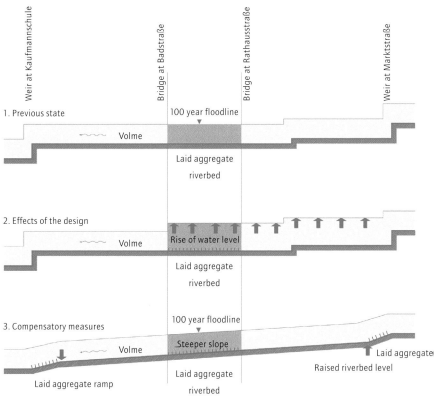

Weir at Kaufmannschule   Bridge at Badstraße   Bridge at Rathausstraße   Weir at Marktstraße

1. Previous state

100 year floodline

Volme

Laid aggregate riverbed

2. Effects of the design

Volme

Rise of water level

Laid aggregate riverbed

3. Compensatory measures

100 year floodline

Volme

Steeper slope

Laid aggregate ramp

Laid aggregate riverbed

Laid aggregate

Raised riverbed level

General plan for the town hall area with complete redesign of the river bed and the water features by the town hall. A crucial feature of the design is to restore accessibility for flora and fauna by rebuilding two weirs.

The Town Hall steps connect the city to the river. The river can be experienced directly thanks to a new path along the river shoreline.

But the people of Hagen seemed most impressed by suggestions for designing the area between the town hall and the Volme. A terrace was to curve along the bank of the river, with enough room for bistro chairs, jutting out over the water in places. From this terrace, a generously dimensioned flight of steps leads down to the gravel shore, and from there it is possible to walk to the next steps. Unless the path is flooded when the river is high. Then a narrow pedestrian bridge will lead from the terrace to the other side of the river. But in Hagen, Herbert Dreiseitl also met the challenge of creating a visible link between the town hall and the river. This was achieved with inlays set in the floor covering and leading to a water wall made of coloured glass, down which water glides. This is the starting-point for a watercourse that takes water from the roof and in a cascade down the steps into the Volme.

To make the terrace and steps part of the town, to remove its backyard image and to give people easier access to the Volme, the floor covering is taken

on into the adjacent street. Even if all this will not really make a great deal of difference to how well people know this industrial town – it has certainly enhanced the quality of life of the people who live there.

A cascade is integrated into the terraced steps. The cascade has an artistic water design which sets the tone for the transition between the urban realm and the natural habitat of the river Volme.

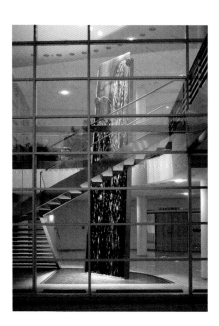

A water wall of glass, water and light within the foyer of the Town Hall extends over two storeys. Particularly at night, the water wall is a distinct symbol visible from the city through the glass façade of the building

Green roof for Chicago City Hall

The flat roof of the historic city hall in downtown Chicago was transformed into a green roof garden.

Many people are familiar with the riveting view from the Empire State Building in Manhattan. Skyscrapers as far as the eye can see, the Hudson River blurs into the horizon, a freedom-loving, copper-clad lady 46 metres high becomes tiny. But at some point the far distance becomes boring and the eye finds its way back and looks down at apparently trivial details: yellow taxis, for example, the winding paths taken by individuals, clouds of pigeons suddenly flying up, the upward and downward staggered patchwork quilt of the flat roofs. Flat roofs are very popular in big American cities. Unlike Central Europe, the airy space in these little rectangles is used for air-conditioning units and fresh water tanks, sometimes for junk. You would look pretty much in vain for a roof garden here. The USA is still a developing country when it comes to roof planting.

Fewer people know the view from the Sears Tower in Chicago, one of the highest office buildings in the world, but if you look down from there it looks quite like the Manhattan roofscape. But this could change very soon, as this great city on Lake Michigan is one of the five major American cities taking part in the environment authority's 'Urban Heat Island Initiative' pilot project. This is the United States' attempt to reduce temperatures in the summer months, which are sometimes very high, and the smog levels in several cities. Roof planting is one of the key elements of this programme, which is also intended to relieve the overloaded sewers when the rainfall is heavy.

There are very few roof-planting experts in the USA because of lack of experience. For this reason the Dreiseitl studio was invited to join an American planning team in 1999, and commissioned to produce a design for a roof area of about 3,600 square metres. And so now people look down from the top of the nearby skyscrapers on to the roof of

Improving the city climate, greening of roof surfaces also significantly reduces rainwater run-off through detention, storage and evaporation of the rainwater.

A natural wildflower meadow right in the middle of Chicago has an aesthetic appeal which is rare in big cities.

the 11 storey town hall. The walls below it are over 100 years old, and familiar to European film fans at least as the notorious Blues Brothers paid their debts there at the last minute.

What has emerged on top of the town hall is a lightly contoured landscape, planted on a shallow substrate with varieties of sedum and on a deeper one with trees and shrubs. It is possible to walk around the city hall roof on a curving path. Parts of the roof were removed for statical reasons before the planting, and provision of water for the roof plants was dealt with as part of this process. Rainwater from the penthouse (for technical units) which is built directly on to city hall, and higher, is stored in several small tanks and taken to the plants when needed. If water is short, the municipal supply can be used.

City hall's green roof has attracted a great deal of attention, and as part of the environment authority's pilot project it has interested specialists, even outside Chicago. In the city itself it is part of the extensive 'City Roof Garden Program', and the first example of the fact that planting on roofs is worthwhile, even from the point of view of economical and sustainable water management.

The garden is visible from the surrounding skyscrapers and has thus become a visual highlight.

The green roof can be enjoyed as a garden oasis from surrounding skyscrapers.

Design for the planted roof: the individual areas form a coherent roof garden.

The Lanferbach at Schüngelberg estate in Gelsenkirchen

Formerly a sewer with sheet-pile walls, the Lanferbach now runs by the Schüngelberg estate in a leisurely fashion.

Overflow of one of the overgrown infiltration swales

The steps by the bed of the stream invite people to stay for a while and play. An old brick wall was used for their construction.

Most of the planners from elsewhere had to get used to two things over the ten years of the International Building Exhibition at Emscher Park: first to the stock of language that had emerged in Germany's melting pot, borrowing all kinds of vocabulary that would otherwise be unfamiliar from the various immigrant groups. And to a kind of person that does not take at lot of things particularly seriously. For example, all the tillefitt, or fuss, about the IBA. Many of these have still not realized that a building exhibition took place in the Ruhr at all, and that countless projects were completed or considered that had a great deal of influence on the local people's living conditions. It is only when your own front garden has been decontaminated or an almost completely natural stream appears instead of a concrete drainage gutter that even the people who didn't particularly care – it was all 'six of one' or 'jacket or trousers', as the German expression has it – that the landscape had taken a turn for the better. It is possible to walk around in it again, to experience it.

One project that became known well beyond the boundaries of the Ruhr is in Gelsenkirchen. A Jugendstil estate in front of the giant Rungenberg spoil heap, also known as Mount Slag, was redeveloped and tastefully complemented with slender terraced housing. The Schüngelberg housing estate for miners had previously been grey, surrounded by dismal green, and bordered by an open, evil-smelling sewer. After redevelopment the complex felt completely different – also helped by attractive open spaces. These appear in the form of nicely proportioned streets, attractive gardens and above all a park which came into being as part of a new rainwater concept. The Lanferbach had previously been a canalized stream in which contaminated water from the Rungenberg slag heap flowed towards the river Emscher. Today the liquid

Before it was redesigned the Lanferbach was forced into a concrete corset and ran through a fenced-off area – 'Danger – No Entry' was the order of the day.

Site management in the mud of Monte Schlacko

Infiltration swale under construction. Water started to accumulate here even in the building phase.

Street water is filtered and purified in retention basins that are integrated into the design, then fed underground to the stream.

Along with the Rungenberg slag heap, which has now been planted, the Lanferbach now functions as a coherent public park area, and is used by the residents for all kinds of activities.

poison flows out of a collective drain into a sewer. This opened up the way for water management in which rainwater from the Schüngelberg estate flows first through various purification stages and retention basins, and is then released in a controlled way into the restored and completely redesigned Lanferbach. Street water runs straight into the retention basins by the Lanferbach and seeps towards the stream through water-bearing strata.

A valuable biotope will develop along a length of just under 800 metres, but this is not all. In fact the estate residents have acquired a new park, which is used a great deal, especially by the large proportion of Turkish inhabitants. Steps intended as seats, built of re-used bricks, draw austere lines in the otherwise gently contoured park landscape. These are the meeting places, which are reached via winding pathways that adapt to the natural design of the park. And the final benefit from the new design is that existing harmful waste was disposed of safely, which at least for the residents of the Schüngelberg estate is not schisskojedno – which is derived from the Polish wszystko jedno, and means roughly the same as 'jacket or trousers'.

The Bridge over the Lanferbach with its discreetly designed steps links the Schüngelberg, the Lanferbach and the Rungenberg slag heap.

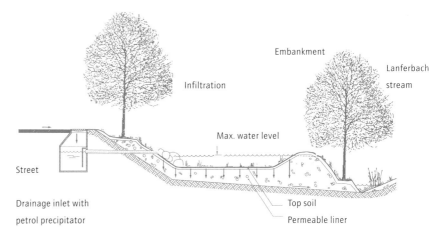

Infiltration

Embankment

Lanferbach stream

Max. water level

Street

Drainage inlet with petrol precipitator

Top soil

Permeable liner

Housing estate in Echallens near Lausanne

The meandering channel is in the central square in the estate, and shows the history of the course of a river with changing loops. At the end a rhythmically pulsating movement is set up that is reminiscent of organic forms (John Wilkes' Flowforms).

Creative people do not always look back on their early work with particular pleasure. We sometimes hear that the artist is pleased to have developed further. This implies an admission that time passes by one's own work as well, that it is subject to fashion – even when designing open space. But ultimate artists are content to know that every work is a step along a path, without which it would not have been possible to reach one's current position – and this alone means that every work is valid in its own right. And as well as this it is enjoyable to see the effect of earlier projects on the thinking of a whole profession, and even on related ones.

This may well be the case for the Dreiseitl studio and the Hameau de la Fontaine estate project in Echallens. In the early 1980s, surface water drainage, swale infiltration, purification in reed beds, installing underground cisterns and re-using rainwater were all seen as newfangled ideas in urban development that people were a little suspicious of. And so it was all the more courageous of the people of Echallens

near Lausanne to commit themselves to an experiment by using a modern rainwater management idea for an estate with ninety dwellings. Since 1986, all the surface water here has flowed along the streets in gutters to a sealed treatment bed. Here the roots of reeds and rushes, in symbiosis with the filter floor, remove the harmful substances from the water before some of it runs into storage tanks. From here water is pumped to the central village well, which is a meeting-place, but also a sculpture, whose impressive volume of flowing water sets currents in motion, whose veil of water reacts to wind, and that is perhaps reminiscent of the fact that the source of all life once sprang from the village fountain. As well as this, a play and adventure area draws its water supply from the tanks. The rest of the rainwater flows into a retention pond, where it evaporates, soaks away or is fed slowly into a stream. The presence of delicate amphibians in the form of alpine salamanders and palmated newts demonstrates the high quality of the water from the reed and rush basins, and also show the importance of artificial water features as second-hand survival biotopes.

It was clear from a very early stage in the Hameau de la Fontaine that how the disciplines of art, open-space architecture, leisure research and environmental technology fuse together to form a single theme.

The centre of the village with a treatment biotope under a platform that is available for performances.

Paved basins show how the rainwater drains away.

Here a second-hand biotope becomes a habitat for creatures under threat, in this case an alpine salamander.

The fountain with its watercourse is a special feature of this estate.

A naturally designed retention pond forms the edge of the estate.

Rainwater management in Krems Business Park, Austria

At times when flooding is on the increase, local authorities think about the omissions of recent years and decades. And they have to do this, as the damage caused by water in recent years have become a regular item in the accounts of local authorities, cantons and states. Unfortunately it is not until it gets difficult to balance the books that ready arguments are available for taking new directions in water management. And here it is important not to be too morose about having to do today what one could have wanted to do yesterday.

The Lower Austrian town of Krems an der Donau demonstrated this in terms of rainwater management. Here the municipal engineers drew up estimates for draining a proposed 33 hectare industrial estate with a conventional sewerage system. But before the community started to implement this, it was well advised to have an alternative concept devised, for open rainwater management. This produced pleasing results. It was possible to use infiltration techniques even for an industrial area in the Danube catchment area with relatively high groundwater levels. Of course the gravelly, sandy subsoil with a Kf value of 1×10^{-3} was of considerable

assistance here. The director of building was particularly pleased when he was able to show a financial saving of over 50 % against the proposed costs for the sewerage solution.

The technical framework for this success lies in a system of long swale strips along the main access road, and infiltration basins between the buildings. Alongside the main access road, the yard and parking areas drain into the decentralized gravel trenches, each complete in itself, after passing through light-density material separators. There are planted retention basins above the trenches. Once the water has arrived here it soaks through a treatment layer about 50 centimetres thick into the gravel trench, which is clad in shear wool, and runs from there into the ground. Roof water flows into planted soakaway basins, and from there into the groundwater. All the sewage is fed into a separate sewer and taken to the communal sewage treatment plant. A relatively large number of roof gardens definitely contribute to the overall efficiency of the concept. Rainwater is delayed in draining from about a third of the buildings. The effects of open infiltration are best studied when rainfall is heavy. The industrial estate has

canals running through it from which water occasionally runs over the edges on to the lawns – but without getting as far as the buildings. But the Landesdorfer Arm, which is linked directly with the Danube, maintains a water level that is well under the top of the embankment. The Krems East industrial estate does not contribute a drop to possible flooding on the Danube and its tributaries.

Constructing a swale system between parking spaces

Gaps in the kerb allow rainwater to run off the streets into the grassed swale alongside and seep away there.

Infiltration via open joints in the pavement

Rainwater concept for the industrial estate showing drainage from roofs and streets and infiltration swales in private and public areas

▨	Roofs
⬚	Planted roofs
Ggü	Green corridor
◌◌◌	Shrubs
⬗	Infiltration swales
▭	Paved surfaces
⊕	Drainage of courtyards with light density precipitators
▱	Retention areas for slow infiltration through planted soil layer for purification
R	Purification bed

A retention basin with infiltration after heavy rain

Grassed swales are placed next to the parking spaces, the trees planted there flourish even in the conditions prevailing in locations of this kind.

Planted swales with a high purification potential for rainwater management

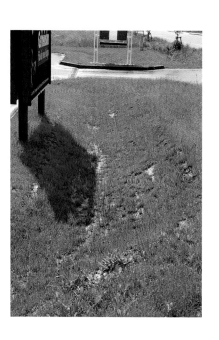

Water as an open system

Wolfram Schwenk

Water is by nature formless and passive, and only shows its particular qualities when interacting with its surroundings. These qualities constitute its significance in the context of nature and teach us to handle water correctly.

Water has become a museum exhibit recently. This gives me pause for thought, as generally speaking museums concern themselves with things that are not (any longer) part of people's everyday experience. And now water in its natural diversity falls into this category, which for me is eloquent evidence of man's alienation from the elemental basis of his life.

We banish water from our environment and allow it to appear for certain purposes only. And so we only perceive it out of context, in specific functions: as a medium between tap and sink, as a drink in a bottle, as rain in the street, as sewage in a sewer, as an attraction in a museum, and in recent years as a flood as well. The links, common to all, archetypal, water's context and its significance in nature are foreign to us. And yet we are talking about the most important basis of our existence, which cannot be replaced by anything else – and not about any old raw material or cultural factor.

Deliberately drawing attention to water has become a cultural activity that would have been difficult to imagine in earlier days. The following remarks about some of water's characteristics are offered to this end.

When trying to describe water using everyday concepts we are immediately confronted with an unexpected problem: as a liquid, water has no shape of its own. It is formless and unconfined, has no hardness or sound of its own – not metallic, not wooden, not bright, not dull. It also has no colour of its own, no smell, no taste of its own.

We also cannot also understand water fully with our five senses: all these can tell us is what it is not and what it doesn't have. And so just as it runs away between our fingers it runs away between our definitions. This is a challenge to reflect and to rethink.

No shape of its own: If water is placed in a container it fills it up and adopts its shape. At the top it always ends as a free waterlevel that adjusts itself to the parallel with the ideal horizon, the surface of the earth. It adapts to its surroundings, down to its very form. If you tilt the vessel, the surface of the water remains horizontal – unlike fixed bodies, whose form is retained when they are twisted and turned. And so for water its situation, its equilibrium is more important that its form – when it is released, it again tries to create a horizontal surface.

No hardness of its own: Water cannot be polished. But you can submerge yourself in it without resistance or throw objects like stones into it. It gives way, accepts these objects and surrounds them.

No sound of its own: When pouring water into a tall glass we notice that the colour and pitch of the sound depend on how full the glass is, in other words on the air-space in the cavity. This also applies to the plashing, murmuring and glugging sound of a brook.

No taste of its own: And yet it is only the moist film of water on our tongues and in our noses that conveys all the nuances to us. We cannot smell or taste anything if our tongue and nose dry up.

Everything that comes into being or passes away, everything that is combined or separated as a material in nature does so only with the aid of water: substances dissolve in it. 'Substances can have an effect only in solution' could be a free re-statement of an old chemical principle. All natural management of substances lives with and on water: in the atmosphere, in the ground, in rocks, and in the waters themselves; in living creatures in breathing and feeding, excretion, regulation, growth, regeneration and reproduction. There is no life without water. Water always mediates, without itself being entirely subsumed in the products of the reactions. It is there to show other things to their best advantage and to convey other things.

As a chemical combination of hydrogen and oxygen, water is defined as H_2O. But pure H_2O does not occur in nature, and not even in the laboratory: in its pure chemical form water is such a powerful solvent that it immediately combines with other substances at the moment it comes into being and dissolves and absorbs at least traces of these. Even the substance we call pure water is always more than H_2O – because it is always open to its surroundings, and is always interacting with them. This is why it is so vulnerable and so in need of protection.

If substances go into solution or are watered down they lose their own form and spatial confinement and gradually fill – together with all the other substances dissolved in it – the whole spatial content of the water that is dissolving them. In their dry and solid form they were distinct from each other within their own forms; now these limitations are lifted and the substances can develop their functional chemical qualities and enter into intimate relationships with each other. In the course of this they adopt an almost weightless condition of floating in the water. Weight loss as a result of buoyancy – divers are always disoriented by the equal pressure from all directions when under water – means being exposed to forces coming from all directions in the surrounding area, a universal balance of forces. Water in water is in this universally open condition.

Running water is a material continuum. It behaves as a coherent whole, not as a material made up of individual particles. And so it does not respond to stimuli in isolation, but always as a whole, systemically. Even minimal shifts in the equilibrium of forces within it set water in motion, and make it flow or pour. Starting at the point where this movement was provoked, fast and slow flowing areas mingle. Along curving or often rolling sections this leads to shearing, in other words partly pulling, partly pushing movements, to blockages and eddying in rhythmic sequence.

Set in motion by interplay with its surroundings, water, which is otherwise so passive, surprises us by producing a whole variety of forms like eddies and waves – and as they come into being they also immediately transform themselves. Every change of movement in water causes shapes to be formed and re-formed, and ultimately these flow away into nothing as soon as they become calm. A game that ceaselessly produces something new, transforms it and takes it back again, a continuous process without a lasting result.

In its material quality water is shapeless, it has no form of its own, but dissolves forms and changes them. It is only movement that makes it a design medium, the scene of an inexhaustible process of renewal, with shapes being ceaselessly formed and transformed, coming into being and passing away.

Many of the development stages of flow formation in water are strikingly similar to organic forms: they can be addressed as organic in terms of their forms. The formative movements that lead to the formation of such currents with their blockages and stretching, overlapping and rolling up in sections with a multiplicity of curves, obey the same laws as the formative movements in the embryonic development of organisms. But something that in an organism becomes the apparently durable condition of the form of a body and its organs through an equilibrium of flow between ceaseless new formation and simultaneous dissolution, remains a formative process in water, and does not acquire a lasting quality. Thus the formative principles of organic and living nature are reproduced as processual events in moving water under the universal conditions of weightlessness and of forces in states that are changing in an unstable fashion. Life-supporting wisdom is woven into these processes. This is – alongside the mediation of metabolism in organisms – the second major sphere in which water works to convey life. Each mingles with the other.

Recent astrophysical research has shown that the laws governing currents in moving water are part of the laws of flow that govern the entire cosmos. The ways the stars relate to each other also follow these laws. And the patterns adopted by the little floating droplets that water forms when falling provide an image of this – they reflect the whole cosmos on a small scale.

In summary: formlessly passive water, mineral according to its material quality, is opened up to the formative forces in living nature by movement. This is shown by the flow patterns that are formed. At the same time they reveal cosmic laws of order: organic laws are also cosmic. The universal laws that form the basis of all life can also be revealed in moving water, and affect it.

Water lives by coming to terms with its surroundings, though excitability, rhythmical articulation in the course of pattern-forming and pattern-changing, and by mediating metabolic processes, and it enlivens those surroundings at the same time.

These qualities of water can be seen in infinite diversity in natural watercourses: in springs and mountain streams it is largely conditions working from the outside – like the structure of the bed, the slope, the daily pattern of light and warmth etc. – that determine the behaviour of water and the absorption and transport of solid and dissolved substances. In big rivers, lakes and in the sea these processes take place to a greater extent inside the masses of water in the form of substance conversion and separation. In meandering streams and rivers on plains these tendencies to absorption, conversion and separation, to shaping and mediating, run in a flow of rhythmical equilibrium. As it comes to terms with the landscape, the course of the river itself becomes an image of these events.

If a creative artist wants to bring about cosmic and organic flow forms in water, this cannot be done in the same way as a sculpture, for example, would be created. They can only be evoked by handling water like an instrument. The creative process then takes place in the water itself. For the artist or designer working with water, this means that he or she makes only part of the work of art. The other, livelier part has to be left to the water – it is to the water that the completion of the work is entrusted. If the artist has learned how water twists and turns as it flows, how it eddies, trickles and spurts, flies and builds up, surges and sloshes, rests and reflects, then some of this can be enhanced and emphasized by creative design, and made into the theme of the joint work of art. Then the designer or artist is working in partnership with the water. This stimulates observers to become aware of the special qualities of water, to discover and experience it, to love it and to value it – and so to learn how to treat it carefully. I know of no better, more attractive and more sustainable ecological study course than this!

A transparent platform for spectators. The use of light and water is carefully cal culated, and here the indi- vidual phenomena and phases are being staged. Suddenly the old wooden gutters under the platform are flooded.

Veils of mist and vapour in the light. Here we are able to see the relationship between the ways in which air and water move.

Natural processes are repeated daily without our knowing exactly what is happening. Do we have a sudden moment of insight when looking at the morning mist or a rainbow, do we know why a drop falls of a leaf at a particular time, and not a moment earlier or later? Unfortunately, being uncertain does not always trigger a thirst for knowledge. Even the most watery problem can sometimes seem too dry, and the chem- istry and physics that could explain it are much too complicated. People like to have answers to their questions, but please make them easy to understand and ideally demonstrated in three dimensions.

When Herbert Dreiseitl demonstra- ted phenomena involving water in the Ruhr city of Gelsenkirchen as part of the Federal Horticultural show in 1997, his intention was to engage and fascinate easy-going people of this kind as well. He found the ideal setting for his experi- ment in showing water in all its states in a cooling tower that had been left standing at the Nordstern pit. After a 15 minute introduction a fine film of water had formed on the spectators' hair and clothes – a perfectly harmless way of acquiring the feeling of being in the middle of a rain-cloud. What had happened? The spectators stood on a glass mezzanine floor, and the develop- ment from mist to a cloudburst was played out before their eyes, with every step in the process accompanied by gigantic slide projections. Every sense was working overtime as first of all their was nothing to be seen in the dark interior of the cooling tower, and then only indirect light, with a bank of mist moving ponderously into position in front of it. Turbulence on the periphery made shining droplets form dancing figures. Slides of foggy landscape thrust into this moving image. Then a circular eddy 1 metre wide rose out of the sea of mist, rather like the smoke-rings blown out by a cigar-smoker in its shape and

The old cooling tower, a relic of the former Nordster pit in Gelsenkirchen, was the scene for a unique presentation of water- related phenomena for over two years.

The magic world of water vapour in an experiment in the old cooling tower

Spectators' stand, slatted frame and the fittings involved in this magical installation

Spectators on the stand
looking up as if spell-bound,
something is going on …

movement. Followed by more rings, it rose to the top of the cooling tower in a cone of light, and then faded away in an air current, along with the clouds of mist. The slide projections of cloud formations appeared on the wall of the cooling tower – there was rain in the air. And it started to fall, first as drizzle, split up into numerous colour zones by beams of light, and then crashing down as an impressive cloudburst. Towards the end the projector revealed another detail: a huge drop of water was getting ready to fall, changing its shape in the first phase of detachment and flight. The demonstration ended with slides of roaring waterfalls – but admittedly not without returning to the cooling tower's original function. The glass platform allowed visitors to see part of the old system of gutters below them filling with water, which then dripped down on to the slatted structure below. Finally we saw how the slats worked to bring about air cooling and make the cooling tower work: the drops of water atomize as they impact, which means that a greater surface area of the water is exposed to the air. The heat in the water is largely dispersed by a stream of air generated by thermal currents, which warms up. It's as simple as that.

The Dreiseitl studio was able to repeat the performance in the IBA presentation year, 1999. The city of Gelsenkirchen wanted to find a long-term operator for the tower – until it was destroyed by arsonists in autumn 2000.

A circular eddy starts to rise from the depths of the cooling tower.

Vapour, mist and smoke remind us of natural and industrial phenomena in the Ruhr.

Spectators can follow the presentation from the glass platform.

Veils of rain and drizzle dance in an air-current in the illuminated cooling tower.

Steel structure
Projectors
Concrete crown

Access gallery
Lattice work
Steel stairs

Elevation and plan
of the cooling tower

Circulation gallery
Valve

Sliding door
Spectators' platform
Access gallery

New entry staircase

Daylighting of Alna River in Hølaløkka, Oslo

The newly daylighted river Alna is followed by a footpath, which in part has pergola niches for lingering and enjoying the river.

Right after the official opening, local residents claimed the park as their own and take particular delight in being able to go for a refreshing swim!

The river Alna is one of the main feeders of the Oslo Fjord. In many parts, the river has been severely degraded. An overall master plan has been developed for the sustainable improvement of the total river watershed area.

A silent consequence of urban expansion, particularly since World War II, has been the disappearance of many small streams from European cities. Culverted out of sight and out of mind of city residents, most streams have ended up as sewer canals. This is the case even in Oslo, capital city of Norway, a country of streams, waterfalls and lakes of enormous natural beauty.

The City Administration realized the extent of growing pollution of Oslo's fjords and increasing pressure on the city watershed. A master plan was developed for the phased restoration of Oslo's biggest river, the Alna, and improvement of the whole greater Oslo watershed area. Atelier Dreiseitl was selected with a local partner, Norwegian landscape architects 13.3, to design and supervise the construction of a pilot demonstration project to generate attention and interest in this long-term and large-scale restoration initiative.

A site located between an industrial business park and a housing estate where a section of the Alna could be day-lighted was identified by the city. A clear aim of the project was to combine a technical water management system, where ecological and hydrological needs were met, with a design that maximizes the potential of an appealing outdoor space. The technical aspects of the water management system are integrated with flair and transparency into the attractive and relaxed atmosphere of the park.

In a more wild and natural corner of the park, the Alna is released into a newly created river bed, which is widened at one point to create a natural settling basin. From here, the stream rounds a corner and feeds into an open swimming pond. Like every river, the flow rate of the Alna can vary significantly with rainfall. A retaining wall on one side of the pond holds back flood waters, specially designed slits allow a reduced outflow with increasing water levels. The adjacent meadow serves the double purpose of an informal relaxing area and a flood meadow. The sum of reducing flooding and increasing water quality in decentralised interventions such as this is the most effective way of achieving the large-scale goals of the master plan.

The retaining wall is a bridge to the other side of the park and the junction point where stormwater run-off from the adjacent industrial park joins the lower part of the system. The roof, surface and road run-off from the industrial park is conveyed via surface drainage detailing to a cleansing biotope (planted sand filter with mineral additives). Intense cleansing and pollutant break-down of the stormwater run-off occurs here, before the water is released to a subsequent wetland area for final polishing. Almost immediately after completion of works, a significant reduction of pollutants was confirmed by city scientists, a trend which is expected to increase and stabilize in the long run. The wetland area also has detention capacity.

The local youths from the adjacent housing estate were the first to discover this new park and turn it into their favourite hang-out.

Behind the park design is an innovative and comprehensive water management concept. A rainwater canal is opened, the water returned to the surface, cleansed and released back into the Alna.

Fountain sculpture in Immenstaad

Stillness and moving
reflections   the sculpture
fountain directly by the
shore of Lake Constance

The sculpture is put in place.

Design sketch:
The sculpture was
cast in bronze.

Arrival and departure – moving moments in man's path through life. And they are particularly striking when there is clearly a long distance ahead of or behind the traveller. Here a town on the sea or a large lake makes coming home or going away most emotional, as one arrives or leaves by ship with deliberation, in the true sense of the word. And there is always a long distance before or behind somebody, in which only water can wash away the last traces.

In Germany, Lake Constance in particular, the country's largest expanse of fresh water, can give the experience of a reasonably long trip by boat. Numerous places on the German, Swiss and Austrian shores receive and say farewell to their residents and visitors – but only a few of them have imposing landmarks to catch the eye. Immenstaad on the north shore used to be one of these. Here the lake widens out to the south-east to the part of it known as the Sea of Baden, and Immenstaad, on a small northern bay, looks south to the majestic chain of the Alps. Over 2 million people a year embark and disembark here.

Since 1991 they have been taking a bearing on a landmark, meeting at a particular place or leaving the little town looking back at a sculpture that is meant to be unforgettable. A landmark on the landing pier, made of stone, bronze and water. A bronze figure 4.5 metres high grows up out of 12 upright stones, local Dornbirn glauconite and Rohrschach sandstone. It faces south, and forms a sensitive point at which the forces of sun, water and wind seem to be concentrated. Its gesture is open to interpretation: water, falling and atomizing according to the strength of the wind gives it a sense of lightness, and can transform rigid metal into a waving flag. It points to the sky, stands in the water, and mediates between the two.

The natural stone steles
are arranged radially.

The individual natural
stones reveal wonderful,
artistically developed
shapes that channel
the water.

Seen with the horizontal breadth of the lake – with the Swiss Alps in the background – the fountain provides a vertical landmark.

Children find little weirs that can be used to regulate the flow of the water back into Lake Constance.

The water collects in a large stepped roundel and then flows, regulated by weirs if necessary, through channels and back into Lake Constance.

On the land side the fountain runs radially in the form of natural stone steles placed on a bed of river pebbles. The location needs a scale of about 300 square metres to develop its full symbolic power and range of uses. 'Free man in the elemental universe' is Herbert Dreiseitl's name for his bronze sculpture. We can believe this – or something completely different. And it is also possible to have different ideas about using the sculpture. The ensemble as a whole is not meant to be just a landmark. It has certainly become a popular meeting-point and place to spend some time. Children like to climb around the steles, and play in the water among the drainage channels with their little weirs, and to use the gravel bed as an area for their own excursions. Adults join in the games, work out the flow patterns of the water on sculpted steles or lose themselves in the visual interplay of distance and proximity. When the lake floods parts of the fountain when the snow melts in summer people are reminded of things that are happening beyond the sculpture, in the far distance. Perhaps a boat is departing for that destination.

The water and wind sculpture in a föhn storm

The lake undergoes dynamic changes in its water level, and so parts of the sculpture disappear with the seasons and then reappear.

The fountain from above. Its radial basic shape is continued in individual stone blocks on the shore of Lake Constance.

Water management for a research centre near London

The building melts into the landscape and is sensitively integrated into the surrounding nature.

The water cascade has a dynamic optic which can be well appreciated from inside the building. The 180 metre long cascade is a major component of the cooling system.

The revolutionary water and cooling system reduces the need for costly technical systems and shows the way for building cooling systems of the future.

The building cooling system is connected to the outdoor water system via a heat exchanger. The collected heat is released to the atmosphere through the cascade and surface of the lake.

Located in a site of unique natural beauty, the building – designed by Foster and Partners – is a transparent glass structure, half-sunken into the hillside to reduce its visual impact. The massiveness of the building is further disguised by a large adjoining artificial lake which wraps like a ying into the yang of the building. Through reflections and surface movements mirrored onto the glass, the building stands with poetic lightness. Atelier Dreiseitl joined the multi-disciplinary design team to advise on combining stormwater management with a water cooling system. There was a very high cooling demand to accommodate. Rather than relying 100 % on conventional cooling towers, it was an environmental and design challenge to define the potential of lake water as a cooling agent, and then optimize it as a highly visible operating system.

The formal lake has a surface area of over 16,000 square metres, and receives stormwater run-off directly from the roof. A 180 metre long, 4 metre high cascade peels out of the building, accompanying the VIP-road, the main access to the building for guests and clients. Whereas the large surface area of the formal lake provides cooling through evaporation, the cascade was specially designed to vapourise the water into small droplets. This serves the multiple purpose of increasing oxygenation of the water, increasing cooling and increasing a white water visual effect. The water is made more visible, and the resulting rhythmic sweeps have an optical dynamism which is particularly refreshing and viewable from the restaurant opposite.

The VIP road turns along the contour of the lake, sloping down with the cascade so that as the cars pull into the entrance they seem to drive over water for the last 40 metres. The water itself is kept in top condition by a 2,100 square metre cleansing biotope. No chemicals are added to the lake. It is essentially a natural water body. In a flexible system designed to accommodate fluctuating cooling needs and optimize water quality, water can be variably extracted from the cleansing biotope and/or the formal lake before being pumped to the heat exchanger. Once through the heat exchanger, the now warm water is returned to the cascade where the cooling cycle begins again. In extreme storm events, the detained overflow can slowly be released into the adjacent Bourne river.

The cascade is constructed from a repeated precast, high-density concrete element. The formal lake is water-proofed with a polyethylene liner. A series of thermal, flow and filtration studies were initially carried out, using computer simulations and numeric calculations. These were important consultation documents during the design process for the entire inter-disciplinary project team.

Center of Excellence, Sindelfingen

The water is circulated through a biotope which cleanses the water with natural effectiveness.

The overview plan shows that the new Center of Excellence is located in a water landscape and is only accessible via a bridge over the water.

Mobility, functionality and dependability are not the only appeal of a luxury car. DaimlerChrysler wanted to create an atmosphere of distinct elegance in the architecture and ambience of their new Center of Excellence in Sindelfingen, reflecting that something extra which defines their new line of Maybach cars.

Water is the medium which connects the new Center of Excellence to the existing Client Center. The water has a mirroring effect, the Center of Excellence appears to glide over the water. To approach the main reception area, visitors cross a narrow bridge which brings them across into the inner area. This crossing of water has always been a movement away from the routine of everyday life.

Thanks to our well-documented and positive experiences at the Potsdamer Platz in Berlin, the client was confident in trusting us to implement a natural and sustainable water system. The waterbody is fed by rainwater collected from the roofs. Without chemicals, in a system which is both ecologically and economically sound, water is circulated in two separate cycles, one for cleansing and the other to reduce stagnant zones in the water body. The cleansing biotope is composed of a sand-gravel substrate planted with wetland type plants. The

The inner space of the building seems to extend out onto the water; the floor level and water level are the same. Views from within the building are greatly enhanced by the water landscape setting.

plants assist in the bonding of phosphates and nutrients and help oxygenate the water. A surface skimmer and trash trap ensure that the water is kept free of larger debris.

Wall elements and window openings give articulated views from the water into the building and vice versa. The soft natural shoreline with attractive planting contrasts with the simple formality of the building, a pleasing juxtaposition which gives the Center a special character.

In counterpoint to the main reception terrace, a water cascade descends to the main water area, the reflections of light and movement imbuing the building walls with the silent vitality of water.

View through the cutout of the wall: the steps of the cleansing biotope are like a cascade and are planted with flowering plants. The wall builds a tension which makes the crossing of the bridge and the view from the terrace even more attractive.

A low-stepped cascade beneath the Maybach Showroom functionally serves as the collection outlet for the water circulation and frames an attractive view from inside.

The Pearl of Hangzhou water garden, Hangzhou

The planned water garden has a romantic radiance paired with sustainable water technology.

Evocative and romantic, West Lake by evening light.

The Pearl of Hangzhou is a precious water pearl on the shores of the famous West Lake.

First impressions from the exit of the pedestrian tunnel: a lively, sparkling water cascade.
The fine-tuned water systems of the cascade and water plaza permanently circulate and cleanse collected rainwater.

The enormous economic expansion and construction boom in China holds the world in suspense. The dimension and tempo of the boom are hard to rival by any western metropolis. When working with the Chinese, one encounters inner values which trigger surprising and unusual lines of questioning for occidentals. Water is valued in China, and respected not only in 'Feng Shui'. Water has great symbolic power which is deep seated in traditional value systems – values which are worth transporting to the modern world of today.

Situated on the upper reaches of the Yangtze Delta only 180 kilometres from Shanghai, Hangzhou is the capital of the Zhejiang province. The Hangzhou district has a population of over 6 million, the city itself is over 1.7 million strong and growing fast. The city government is trying in many areas and projects to preserve and renew traditional urban culture and structures while meeting the needs of a demanding, expanding modern city.

In every season, the West Lake is the jewel of Hangzhou, and offers romance and mysticism to the delight of its visitors. Yet the quantity of tourists and the demands of agricultural, industrial and domestic outfall have noticeably influenced the water quality of the lake for the worse.

Impressed by the success of Xintiandi in Shanghai (a shopping/restaurant centre tastefully built in modern renovated traditional Chinese architecture), the City of Hangzhou invited the same developers, Shui On Properties, to tackle a large site right on the lake front. The three phase project includes a romantic park island, an urban shopping village and a citizens water plaza. Together with Architects Wood + Zapata and civil engineers Ove Arup, Atelier Dreiseitl developed water concepts for all three phases of the project and in particular the citizens water plaza, called the Pearl of Hangzhou Water Garden.

In Phase 1, the park island, the rainwater concept is to collect run-off from the roofs and use it for irrigation of the park and toilet flushing in the amenities. The whole of Phase 2, the urban shopping village, is pedestrian. Water is collected from the pedestrian streets and roofs and used to supplement water cascades and walls, which are conceived to greatly improve the indoor/outdoor climate comfort of the village. The remaining rainwater is stored to be used for cleaning the pedestrian streets, which due to expected visitor numbers will be washed down up to twice a day. A dramatic water cascade shimmers in the light and draws visitors through an underground pedestrian passage to the West Lake and to the Pearl of Hangzhou water garden. This is a landscape of play and stimulation of the senses. At the centre of a dynamic spiral, a 'pearl' sprays cooling water during the day and glows with sensual colours during the night. A demonstration fountain extracts dirty water from the West Lake, circulates it through cleansing biotopes before returning it to the lake, showing a green technology which could be used on a greater scale to improve the quality of the lake.

The implementation of the project is dependant on a complex net of political considerations. Great respect is due to the city which is seeking to balance through this outstanding project the economic prosperity of its businesses with real quality of life for its citizen.

Towards a new water culture

Detlev Ipsen

We are going to have to learn how to handle water in future. This means co-operative planning and a high level of participation. A project in Hannoversch Münden has produced some early experience in this field.

If you ask people about environmental problems in surveys, water is almost never mentioned. More of them are aware of traffic, noise and air pollution and the hole in the ozone layer. We carried out surveys in Dresden and Frankfurt in which only 7.6 % of the Dresden residents questioned mentioned water as an environmental problem, and in Frankfurt it was only 3.3 %. We need to drink water every day, and use it to keep clean, to promote a sense of well-being, and for recreation. So why is it not watched with particular care in respect to possible environmental problems? How can this be explained?

Obviously the fact that water is generally and constantly available, naturally and through technology, the frequent precipitation in our latitudes, full streams and rivers, and running water in our homes all seem to give the lie to the idea that water could be a problem. Anyone who looks at the world a little more closely knows how the deserts are spreading, remembers the droughts in the Sahel and Somalia, and has heard about conflicts over the waters of the Jordan and the Euphrates. But why should water be a problem in Central Europe?

In fact the water problem in Europe is not a problem of quantity, as a rule, even though water represents the greatest flow of any material through our cities. The principal problem in Central Europe is not a general shortage, but a shortage of water of outstanding quality, and the pollution of waterways, which goes far beyond the point at which streams or rivers can clean themselves. Obviously in recent decades people have become accustomed to the fact that rivers are not suitable for bathing, or springs for drinking. Even tap water is distrusted. Over 84 % of people never or seldom drink water from the tap.

And so the water problem is first and foremost a problem of quality. The quantity problem comes second. Groundwater pollution has accustomed people to the fact that large cities can draw only a tiny proportion of their water from their own territory, and so use supplies from further away. In any case, poor groundwater quality means considerable expense for treating and transporting water, and often triggers regional conflicts. Then pressure groups demand reduction of the quantities drawn and a more sophisticated handling of water.

The current argument runs that anyone who air-conditions offices with best-quality drinking water, cleans cars and flushes toilets with it, is lowering groundwater levels and causing damage frivolously, not as a matter of necessity. Political pressure can be exerted on towns and cities to be more aware and economical in their use of water by articulating the problems in the areas where it is drawn. But why are people not acutely conscious of the problem despite high costs, possible damage and the risk of endangering health?

The search for an answer to this question leads to the issue of the structure of the modern city. Its development began with the cholera epidemics which haunted many European cities in several waves during the 19th century. At this time and also in the wake of major urban planning changes, such as initiated in Paris by Georges Eugène Haussmann, water pipes were installed.

The shock caused by the cholera epidemics has had a far greater effect than containing and controlling the epidemics themselves. The construction of sewerage systems and the piping of drinking water to individual houses and flats, the gradual spread of private toilets, the establishment of public bathing facilities which then also became more widespread in private houses, did not just build up a general culture of hygiene, but fundamentally changed the relationship between the city and its citizens. Many of the vital processes of urban life were put under state control in the course of this development and offered by municipal utilities to citizens as a compulsorily imposed service. This did not just apply to water supply and waste water disposal, but also to food supply in new abattoirs and covered markets built and controlled by the police, waste disposal, voluntary or compulsory health care and state epidemic policies, down to the control of private living conditions by state housing inspectors.

What does all this mean in terms of the way problems are perceived in towns?

Firstly, many aspects of everyday life were withdrawn from civil authority and handed over to state and municipal bureaucracies. The transformation to the civilized modern town was in fact a process of 'de-civilization'. Household and neighbourhood responsibilities for water supply and faeces disposal were taken over by bureaucratic institutions.

Secondly, most of the technical and natural side of this process becomes invisible to ordinary citizens. An individual household cannot possibly see where the water comes from and where it runs away to, and the same applies to food and energy. Significant elements of urban life are no longer directly visible. Hence experience of the natural and technical context of urban life is lost, and new experience of this kind cannot be gained. At the same time responsibility for and thus relation to material elements is becoming increasingly disparate, and on the expert plane this cramps the way in which things are seen.

So the water problem extends to two poles: the material side, which presents itself as a threat to the quality of the resource, and the social side, which is categorized by a loss of awareness of the problem. Both poles are very closely connected with the development of the modern city, where a technical administrative infrastructure has been built up so that the city's natural side can be regulated as efficiently as possible. If we see the emergence of this infrastructure as the 19th century's reply to the environmental crises identified at the time, then the perceptual distance from 'nature' is the 20th century social consequence of this piece of problem-solving.

We use the concept of 'water culture' to relate the various aspects of water, and thus also of water problems, to each other. Usually the idea of culture is linked with the culture business, with theatre and museums, cinema and concerts. It is also used in a quite different sense from day to day. We talk about a cooking culture, or planning culture, and refer disparagingly to an uncultured attitude. Systematically speaking, the idea of culture has an analytical and a normative aspect. We understand culture to be the meanings and senses that permeate one or more realms of the material and social world. When we speak of water culture we are referring to the meanings and senses that relate to water as a material, to water technology, to the aesthetics of water and to the various social ways of dealing with water. But water culture also includes the interpretations and meanings associated with water. The concept of culture helps us to understand the different aspects of water in their relationship with each other. Just as Roman culture was not made up merely of the Latin language and the writings of Seneca, but also of the roads and aqueducts of the Roman Empire, in the same way water culture includes legal standards, water technology, water economics and social ways of handling water in one meaningful relation. So we do not mean that there would not be a water culture today, but that the water culture that is predominant today could be changed if we try to deal with water in a sustainable manner.

We understand sustainable water culture as a 'culture of many waters'. Today as a rule the same water is used for making tea, taking a shower or washing the car. A sustainable water culture would have different water available for different purposes. One and the same lot of water will be put to work in different ways in use cascades. Streams in towns will no longer be drainage ditches and sweep faeces and refuse past the sewage treatment plants into the rivers when it is raining heavily. Rivers will be used for irrigation, for bathing, for sport and for recreation, thus enhancing the value of the landscape outside our front doors.

Prices for water and sewerage services have risen considerably more than the average cost of living in recent years. And the new sustainable water culture will not get any cheaper. This will also need care to be taken by ordinary citizens, as well as by the 'professional water suppliers'. It is not just the local authorities and the state that will be responsible, but everybody. This will also not be simple, even if it is possible to imagine fluent transitions from volunteer to paid work.

Ordinary citizens are only likely to take responsibility for water, and higher charges for developing a sustainable water culture will only be accepted, if people are aware of the value of water. One, perhaps even the most important, way of conveying this value is the natural and designed aesthetic of water. Pleasure in water conveyed by the senses and reflection about the condition of water stimulated by the senses are paths to sustainability.

Fortunately this is not all just a pipe-dream or a piece of woolly-headed idealism, but a great deal of it has already been set in motion, and a lot of people are working on keeping it in motion. Of course this is not a simple path, and there are many questions to be answered: can we afford ecology? Are ecology and urban life contradictions in terms? Do town-dwellers want to address, or better, under what conditions can they address, ecological urban redevelopment? How can ecology become a guideline for future cities? What do ecological aesthetics mean in concrete terms? Finally all these questions boil down to one key question: how can ecology be fixed in town-dwellers' minds as a meaningful project?

The town of Hannoversch Münden is addressing these questions with the 'Wasserspuren' (Water-Traces) project. Three central squares around the church and the town hall are to be designed in such a way that the qualities of water can be experienced visually and acoustically. The town is between the rivers Fulda and Werra, and its history has been affected both for good and ill by these rivers. It is creating a new interpretation of its relationship with water as part of the natural environment. Traditionally urban squares, as something shaped and designed by man, are set against the ultimately uncontrolled nature of rivers. Now they are to convey the ecology of the whole habitat, of the city and of nature, to the townspeople.

New planning approaches have to be taken if a project of this kind is to succeed. The less conventional and tried-and-tested the aims of a piece of planning are, the earlier the well-trodden paths of planning have to be abandoned. Planners and architects, artists and townspeople start to co-operate on developing and implementing the project. Planners, artists and townspeople developed planning suggestions in joint workshops, under an outside chairman who was familiar with the town and its characteristics. These ideas were then put to a jury of external experts and local politicians. This was intended to produce high-quality designs and also to develop co-operation between the planners and artists involved. In this way the initiators of the process hoped that the townspeople would not just be involved in developing concepts and plans, but they would be protagonists in their own right, and thus also disseminators of the planning idea. Politics and administration create the general conditions needed for this process.

We call this kind of planning 'deep participation'. But it does not just go beyond the boundary between citizen and planning, but also beyond the boundary between the various views taken by the involved. Artists, landscape designers, architects and townspeople work in a team, without changing or confusing their roles. Administration and politics admit an open process, with results that are often surprising. The political culture also benefits from the fact that politicians and administrators prove they are open to discussion.

The townspeople were informed – at first via the local press, then at meetings intended to provide information – about the new design and the possibility of being actively involved in the process themselves. Shortly before the protagonists' first plenary meeting a good third of all the people of Hannoversch Münden knew about the new project they were about to be involved in. Private individuals working with artists and planners in so-called planning workshops were the key point of the active participation. These workshops were intended to come up with a joint design concept. The suggestions were examined and reported on by a jury of outside planners and local politicians or members of the administration, and then 'returned' to the planners and artists for revision, with suggestions and corrections. The participating townspeople could also familiarize themselves with other groups' ideas during the workshops. If a process like this is successful, the townspeople who are actively involved can also help to disseminate the ideas that the other planning teams come up with.

But the innovative potential is essentially to be found in the constellation of townspeople-planners-artists as an active group. A constellation of this kind, with the minimum involvement possible by politicians, administrators and the other usual interested parties, really is new. At the design phase in particular it is relieved of pressure from the particular interests that usually impinge upon planning processes.

By the time EXPO 2000 opened, the town's newly designed squares were ready to be assessed by the townspeople and visitors. We asked a representative cross-section of townspeople for their opinion of the new design.

In reply to the question 'What do you think about each of the squares?', in the case of Kirchplatz 60.9 % said 'pleasant', 21.1 % 'unpleasant' and 18 % were indifferent. The equivalent figures from the poll in September 1997 were 54.6 %, 10.6 % and 26.8 %. In the case of the intermediate square, 56.6 % of respondents were positive about the design, 21.5 % negative and 21.9 % indifferent. Three years before the same question had produced proportions of 15.8 %, 39.5 % and 44.7 % respectively. And finally for Rathausplatz, in 2000 65.3 % of respondents reacted positively, 19.9 % negatively and 14.7 % indifferently. In 1997 the equivalent figures were 70.9 %, 8.2 % and 20.9 %.

If we compare the surveys taken in 1997, when the squares were in their original condition, it is clear how much the townspeople's opinion differs. In the case of Rathausplatz, which in 1997 was in a condition acceptable to the townspeople, the renewal of the pavement, shifting the market to this square and including it in the 'Wasserspuren' project met with a positive response from most people, but this group has become smaller. There are now also more people who find the reconstructed square unpleasant. In the case of Kirchplatz, which has been clearly redesigned and makes an unambiguous reference to the theme of 'Wasserspuren', there is more general approval. The highest level of acceptance is found in the intermediate square that has changed from being a municipal bus-stop to an aquatic urban space.

Two things are clear here. There is not a great deal of additional gain to be had from a base where acceptance levels are already high. On the contrary, supporters of the old conditions turn against the 'new' design in greater numbers. Secondly the key thematic design, in this case the idea of 'Wasserspuren', seems to have been convincing. And this increases in proportion with the unpopularity of the square in its old state.

Ecological aesthetics are not always successful even when townspeople are profoundly involved in the planning process. But firm commitment to the theme is probably the way to broaden identification to the greatest possible extent.

'Water-traces' in Hannoversch Münden

The lighting design generates always new perspectives in the water.

People wonder about the source of major rivers from time to time. And there are some that do not have a source at all. The Weser, for example. It seems that it got its name because people could not agree whether the river should be called the Fulda or the Werra from the point at which they meet in Hannoversch Münden. This town, now called Hann. Münden for short, is near Kassel, and – as is the case with many places on rivers – water is very important, bringing great happiness and great misery. And yet the two rivers that meet here flow past behind the old town, and are quite insignificant for it and in the awareness of many people.

A well as three rivers, the town also has three connected squares in the heart of the old quarter: Kirchplatz, the square between the church and the town hall and the market-place. When decisions were made about traffic-calming, people had the idea of redesigning and revitalizing the squares. A theme was quickly found: 'water-traces' – the paths followed by watercourses – were to be made visible. Registering as an associate Expo location provided an immovable completion deadline.

The way in which project was organized made a major contribution to its success. Five working groups made up of residents, landscape architects and fine artists, chaired by an architect, developed a wide range of ideas. Experts worked together and with laymen in an open atmosphere and finally created six works of art in the ensemble of squares, which slopes downwards from south to north.

The Dreiseitl studio built its contribution to this system, which is fed mainly by rainwater, in the square between the church and the town hall. There are four terraced steps here, like a large folded carpet. The water bubbles out of the topmost, narrowest terrace, and runs over the next three, each of which drops through a small height.

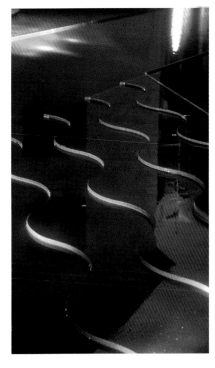

Three ramps between the fields reveal the rhythmic flow patterns on the surface of the water.

The rhythmic patterns on the surface of the water are reflected on to the large town hall façade by cleverly devised lighting management.

A narrow stainless steel gutter accepts the water at the bottom and takes it back to the circulation tank. And now people of all ages can go in search of the traces left by the water on this carpet. One aspect is that the water leaves all sorts of different traces because of differences in the subsoil. But then people can leave their own traces or tracks here – which was very important to the artists and planners. The nature of the flow is changed if people simply step into the pool. But you can also change the flow pattern by using the plates, slides and wave-making devices that are placed around the carpet.

Experience, touch and just get going and play without worrying

The sounds of the city are collected by a microphone that is integrated into the wall and then transformed into vibrations of the metal plate. The plate thus becomes a special interactive element.

The shallow water allows for playing on the water 'carpet'. Three steles with light and sounds accentuate the square.

The overall effect is further enhanced by three steles: V-shaped glass about 5 metres high sits on a steel plinth and is lit obliquely after dark. Light is then caught by a sand-blasted relief, and produces an image. Light then shoots in its turn through the gap in the V to the mirror at the top, which casts the beam on to the pool of water whose mobile structure is then reflected on to the wall of the town hall. Loudspeakers mounted in the steles throw artistically alienated voices or sounds made by water out into the scene, as a pattern of urban noise. Here water is clearly making a material effect. Flow images trigger ideas, projections give rise to associations, water leaves traces.

Interior courtyard of an old people's home in Stuttgart

Water glides softly through stone channels, makes a pleasing sound in little waterfalls then disappears again among the aquatic plants. The sound brings a sense of magic to the space, and life into the old people's home.

The natural stones have been treated artistically, the gliding wave structures swirl like pennants.

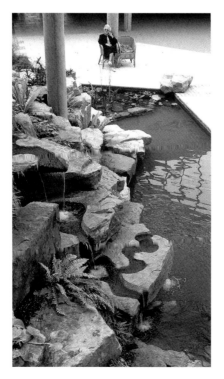

For people who like to have greenery around them the Nicolaus-Cusanus-Haus in Stuttgart offers an internal space with a lot of plants, thus bringing nature even to those who are confined and can only control how they spend their own time to a limited extent: the occupants of old people's homes and nursing-homes. The first impression is that of being in the tropical house in a botanical garden, though without the greenhouse atmosphere that quickly drives Western Europeans back out into the fresh air. This idea comes from a luxuriant display of mainly evergreen plants, in a glazed inner courtyard covering 800 square metres.

Water is the crucial element that creates the atmosphere of this space. It is first noticed on the level of sound: the splashing and glugging creates a comfortable acoustic background. But water makes its biggest effect here because of the surfaces it runs down, from which it drips and over which it runs away. All these features are made of stone and discreetly sculpted. Long horizontal scales are worked into steeply sloping lumps of stone, and the water drips down these, leaving some parts dry and allowing various kinds of moss to grow. Natural stone blocks were piled up, and Herbert Dreiseitl had meandering and branching grooves chiselled and cut into them. The water flows through them as if it had made these pathways for itself, and finally ends up in troughs and basins after running under little bridges and washing around stepping stones. The inner courtyard of the Nicolaus-Cusanus-Haus has set new standards for old people's living conditions, indeed for humane living conditions. The residents enjoy expansive views of terraces, steps and paths on four storeys, or can sit in sheltered alcoves away from it all. They feel at home in temperatures between 18 and 25 degrees – and also that they are being cared for in a very special way.

The courtyard offers changing perspectives.

Heiner-Metzger Plaza, Neu-Ulm

The participation of school children from design to construction is the key to the success of this project.

The plaza design springs from the idea of creating different use zones as islands. There are islands for rest and for activities under the trees. The hard, urban plaza edge is turned to the street where the fountain is both a highlight and a screen against passing traffic.

On many issues Neu-Ulm is overshadowed and out-muscled by her elder, bigger sister, Ulm. The two cities are physically separated by the river Danube and politically by the state boundary; Neu-Ulm is in Bavaria, Ulm in Baden-Württemberg. Ulm is a historic town, severely bombed during World War II. Neu-Ulm was largely constructed after the war and retains the character of a suburb, rather than a town in its own right. This is however a unique (now 'historic') urban style and has a rough, strangely appealing charm. The Neu-Ulm train station was demolished and put underground, which opened the opportunity for a signature urban renewal project, the redesign of the Heiner-Metzger Plaza in front of the former train station. This is part of a larger scale inner city renovation and expansion project, connecting Neu-Ulm to the Danube waterfront and given additional impulse by the State Garden Expo planned for 2008.

Neu-Ulm's dynamic mayor did not hesitate to get town citizens in on the action. In particular, high school students were included in a design workshop, coordinated by Atelier Dreiseitl but planned by the students themselves, after which they went on to further develop the project with their teachers and the city planning department. Instead of abstract, political intellectualism, young adults respond to facts, and express themselves with emotion and feeling, when they are given the chance to get involved. The themes 'a meeting point for generations' and 'fun space' started to crystallize. Climbing, chess, games, corners and other ideas started to flow for a place with a contemporary concept of 'leisure' – active, moving, dynamic, and in every case including water.

The students were then invited for a workshop at Atelier Dreiseitl. Water phenomenon experiments were used as an ice-breaker for minds and voices.

Collection, filtration and infiltration of stormwater

Activities for all generations

The water feature is a space sculpture which maintains transparency through the fine stainless steel meshes. Set with changing water flows, the screens alternate between being transparent and forming a soft visual barrier. They are also a sound set, pushing back the noise of the city.

Models were built, sketches were drafted and redrafted, and discussions were held with unforgettable intensity.

Atelier Dreiseitl took all this input and synthesized it into a final design based on use zones. An internal corner has a compacted gravel floor and is sheltered by trees. This is an active play area with a funky climbing wall, resilient table football and outdoor chess. An edging wall provides abundant seating. The external corner, bounded by the two roads, is an ensemble of water screens. These are a highly visible identity marker, subtly and transparently shielding the plaza from traffic with suggestive views cut through. They define an inner space, which is active and fun with changing water patterns and intensities. The gurgling noise of the water creates a 'soundscape'. Through another physical sense, the inclusiveness and fun atmosphere of the plaza is reinforced. Seating blocks were designed by students and sited together in the 5 centimetre shallow water screed.

Stormwater run-off from the plaza is collected, filtered and then infiltrated in constructed layers of gravel under the paving. Instead of using environmentally and financially expensive potable water, ground water is used to supplement the circulation systems of the water features. A cycle of responsibility is established between the site and ground water.

Local industries were drawn into the tide of enthusiasm and donated construction materials. The good press reviews felt like a reward for everyone especially after all the hard work that went into the project. Inclusion and acceptance by the local youth is the ultimate safeguard against vandalism. So far the new Heiner-Metzger Plaza is proving the worth of a community inclusive planning process.

Exemplary water management at DWR Headquarters, Amsterdam

For a dyke control and sewerage utility company in Amsterdam, expectations are high in regards to the stormwater management of its own sites, plants and buildings. DWR Amsterdam intended to meet and exceed these expectations with the design and construction of its new headquarters on the River Amstel, setting an example for excellent water practice.

The new building is fronted by a large water basin, with one of the two high-rise towers propped directly above the water. The basin is multifunctional. On one hand, it detains stormwater run-off from the site before slowly releasing it to the river Amstel. On the other, without a liner or artificial sealing, it is open to ground water and acts as a collection reservoir for water to be used for toilet flushing, cleaning and air-conditioning. The water level of the basin can fluctuate significantly. All of these variables necessitate the maintenance of sufficiently high water quality.

Atelier Dreiseitl designed the detailed operation system and shaped the aesthetic character of the water basin. Form, depth and water flow patterns were analysed, so that an optimised functional system could be seamlessly integrated into the aesthetic fine-tuning of the basin. In terms of the aesthetic handling of the basin edges and the overall cleansing requirements, the 30 centimetre fluctuating water level posed a particular challenge. Two different types of cleansing biotopes were installed at opposing sides of the basin, and terraced down from maximum to minimum water levels. Different plants reflect different cleaning functions, give the basin scenic variety and intimacy, and ensure that the water remains sufficiently clean at all times and water levels.

The main entrance to the building is tantalizingly suspended over the water.

Although visually evident, a more sensual connection is made by a proposed indoor water curtain, which through sound, light and a cooling sensation brings an awareness of water inside the building. Visitors are bathed in the impression of cool, fresh water. For DWR, it is a celebration of the achievement of large-scale sustainable water management reflected within the microcosm of their new headquarters.

A detailed circulation concept was developed responding to the challenge of varying water levels.

Cleansing biotopes with flowering wetland plants ensure good water quality.

A rainwater concept for the administrative headquarters of DWR is to set an example in Amsterdam for sustainable rainwater management.

The Emscher today – simply an open sewage channel

Industrial regions such as the Ruhr Valley, one of Europe's biggest industrial conglomerations with a population just under 4 million, have decidedly improved the level of affluence and comfort of our Western civilization.

In many incidences, this industrial improvement has been at the cost of the environment and natural resources, and many healthy rivers have been sacrificed along the way. 100 years ago, the river Emscher wound its way through an intact river meadow and wetland habitat. As a consequence of coal mining, the land sunk and the river Emscher came to serve as sewerage and general rubbish canal. The result was regular and putrid flooding. In those days, the solution was to build dykes and fortified river walls. This only intensified the impression of an open sewer canal, a 'cloaca maxima', on whose shores one did not willingly loiter. Although right in the middle of the urban conglomeration, the once lovely river meadows became a place to avoid.

Structural changes in industry and impulses drawn from the International Housing Exhibition IBA Emscher Park 1990–1999 have given orientation to new cultural and industrial movements where the river Emscher is the central focus.

Today, the Emschergenossenschaft, Germany's largest Sewer Management Association, is proceeding together with cities, industries and riverside occupiers on a regeneration project of the Emscher. The total investment volume is over 4.2 billion Euro, and the project includes vastly more than just river habitat restoration. It is a once-in-100-year-chance for the region.

First steps include rebuilding superannuated sewer canals and many decentralized sewer treatment plants to ensure that all waste water is effectively and properly cleaned before it reaches the river Emscher. Most importantly, rainwater will be, as far as possible,

According to the new concept, rainwater from the stadium and parking lots is collected, cleaned and slowly released back into the restored Emscher.

Nightlife with illuminated water-traces in front of the Westfalen Stadium.

The island between the Rhein-Herne Canal and Emscher has development potential for an 'Emscher-Info-Park' and also being integrated into the surrounding urban fabric.

Water themes can also be humorous – for instance football!

Reconstruction of the complete sewage and rainwater network of one of Europe's biggest urban conglomerations along 60 km of Emscher riverfront.

Waltrop

Recklinghausen

Herten

Gelsenkirchen

Gladbeck

Bottrop

Castrop
Rauxel

Oberhausen

Herne

Duisburg

Dortmund

Bochum

Essen

Section of the island between the Rhein-Herne Canal and the river Emscher.

disconnected from the underground sewerage canal network, and conveyed on the surface. Here it can be detained, cleansed and then released slowly into the Emscher. The goal is, within the next 15 years, to get every drop of rainwater fed into the river for 15 % of the total project area.

The Atelier Dreiseitl team is working on several pilot projects which will get this enormous undertaking started. One of these projects is the Westfalen Stadium in Dortmund, where numerous games are to take place during the 2006 Football World Cup. Rainwater run-off from the stadium roof and huge parking lots is collected in 'treatment trains', where the water can be cleansed, detained and from there slowly released into the nearby Emscher. The route of the rainwater is made visible and understandable to football fans and passers-by. It becomes an environmental theme, which in addition to football, characterises the stadium.

In numerous housing areas, industrial parks and public facilities, the new, sustainable path of rainwater is being made visible and aesthetically appealing. It is to become an integrated quality in the urban character. To communicate the totality and details of the overall project, a former water treatment plant, on an island between the Emscher and the Rhein-Herne Canal, is being rejuvenated as an information centre. The redesign and regeneration of the Emscher watershed area affects every resident and needs every resident's motivation to get through the

next 25 years of anticipated reconstruction. Seeing the pilot projects realised in the near future will provide some of the stamina and patience which local citizens, businesses and industry will need to see this visionary project through.

Former settling basins become the setting for temporary art installations. The 60 kilometres of restoration projects are communicated within a treatment plant turned information centre.

The old sewage treatment plant has been retired and is now being reincarnated as an 'Info-Park': the future brings new life.

Water playground in Pforzheim

Children like asking questions, and sometimes they ask a lot. Adults don't always like explaining things, rarely do it vividly and sometimes not at all – if they don't know the answer. This is why children's playgrounds exist. They can look for things to do there, set themselves problems and work out how to solve them. Water is always on the move, creates a path for itself, comes to the surface, collects, seeps away – and raises questions. How does water come to the surface, why does it flow in the way it does, where do I stand in the cycle of coming to the surface and running away?

A water playground in the South German town of Pforzheim tries to provide answers to these many questions. It stands on the northern edge of the Black Forest, and in 1992 staged the regional horticultural show, using a very varied landscape featuring all aspects of water in an area of 4,000 square metres. 'Learning through play', an appeal from progressive educationalists, is something that is done here by children and a large number of adults as well. And in two contrasting spheres: nature and civilization.

In the natural section the water appears in gently modelled brooks flowing through meadows and irrigation areas. The water rises from various clefts in a round stone basin or emerges as a surface spring from the luxuriant growth around basins on the site, then flows on its way, by now a little brook, to the civilization section. There it splashes, twists and winds through everything relating to water technology's evolution history. Ancient devices for raising water (the Egyptian shadoof), Archimedean screws, a medieval well-shaft and a rotary pump are arranged together in a chain of play-stations. Visitors can and should play in both zones, but while tranquillity is the key feature of the natural area, fun and games are the order of the day in the civilized zone.

Herbert Dreiseitl had the water-raising devices arranged in such a way that it is almost impossible to resist a water-drawing competition. For example, of the four Archimedean screws, two are placed at the top and two at the bottom, so that two teams of two can play at raising water on to the higher level. In this upper channel, into which the other raising devices also drain, the water continues on its way to a play castle. Here water comes to the surface again, and flows away in various directions when retention weirs are opened and closed, to an experiment channel or an aqueduct. All these play-stations have turned out to need little maintenance over the years.

The water playground is in precisely the right place between the little river Enz and the historic waterworks. A proportion of about 20 % of fresh water is introduced into the cycle from the waterworks, to meet the purity requirements. The playground is near the city centre, and has drawn visitors in large numbers ever since it opened. This is probably due to the generous provision of busy and quiet areas and its unique character, which is also expressed in all the play-stations, each of which is unique in its own right. Here asking questions can turn into a game.

The ancient devices for raising water, Archimedean screws and the shadoof in the background teach history through the medium of play.

A water playground by the river – here everyone can join in. Water can be raised, played with and experienced.

The lockkeeper at the moated castle gives permission to proceed – a water-channel with mobile obstacles, research into water behaviour in the playground

The medieval well-shaft, discovered by children working as a team

Dieter Grau, Alexander Edel, Gerhard Hauber, Herbert Dreiseitl

From the idea to the finished object

Section through
purification biotope

Water basin

Main inflow

Inflow gutter

Inflow basin 3

DN 200

428.90

+0.47 (428.67)

WSP +0.47 (428.67)

+0.87 (428.87)

+0.27 (428.47)

+0.40 (428.60)

Abdichtung +0.17 (428.37)

WSP −0.03 unter OFF (428.17)

− 0.43 (427.77)

Water can be a problem in urban open spaces. Building water features seems prohibitively expensive, too many things can go wrong, and maintenance is too expensive. But when the water quality is right, pumps, filters and control devices are working properly, the parts of the building that come in contact with the water are not damaged and when water, along with light and sound effects, turns boring places into exciting ones, no one wants to be without it. But however easily and light-heartedly water flows and splashes – it needs expert handling in urban landscapes.

Constructed water features are always individual objects. They emerge from interplay between the possibilities offered by the site and clients' and planners' ideas and wishes. The techniques used to install and run them are as varied as the water features themselves. They are rarely to be had off the peg, but need a technical concept that is individually tailored to their location.

But on the other hand there are always standards and guidelines to be taken into account, for example those applying to the depth of the water or water hygiene. There are a wide range of regulations applying to these in different countries. Experience shows that these can be interpreted individually in terms of each particular situation. This is especially true if new and unconventional ideas are being realized: it is innovative concepts above all that mean thinking beyond existing norms. Here the key recommendation is that the responsible

authorities should be involved in the search for new solutions from the outset.

The following brings together a few hints on building and running water features that have emerged over the years from day-to-day work in the studio.

Sourcing and water quality

A fundamental criterion for the building and running of water features is the quality of the water. This is affected by physical, chemical and biological processes in the water itself and by its interplay with its immediate surroundings.

Water sourcing: Water features usually tap into the local water supply which generally means using drinking water. It is also becoming increasingly attractive to think of using available surface run-off, drainage water or roof collected rainwater.

The origins and quality of water are crucial in terms of its possible use. When concerning a complex planning task, it is advisable to consult experts like limnologists to develop parameters for anticipated water quality. It is also important to identify questions about water hygiene and upkeep as quality requirements even during the design phase. Different standards apply according to the purpose for which the water is being used. The more the water comes into direct contact with people, for example with children playing, the more

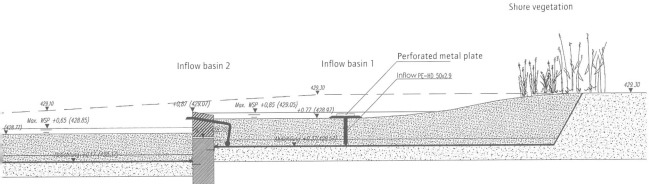

Shore vegetation

Inflow basin 2　　Inflow basin 1　　Perforated metal plate

Inflow PE-HD 50x2.9

429.30

429.10

+0,87 (429.07)　Max. WSP +0,85 (429.05)

+0.77 (428.97)

429.30

Max. WSP +0,65 (428.85)

(428.77)

Abdichtung +0,57 (428.57)

(428.77)

drinking water or at least bathing water quality will be required. As a rule water features that suggest drinking, in other words raised features, should use drinking water, while bathing water quality is usually sufficient for features at ground level, or for pools.

The interplay between water and its built environment should be taken into account at the planning stage. Materials like concrete or mortar can have a significant effect on water chemistry, increasing the calcium content and raising the pH value of the water drastically. This can have a very negative effect on flora and fauna and in extreme cases damage the surface of materials.

Certain nutrients and germs will get into the water naturally by rainfall and can cause biological surface growth like algae or bacteria. The aim should be to keep this within tolerable bounds. Unrealistic expectations on the part of the client, like clear water that is free of algae at all times, should thus be discussed in advance. Such a requirement makes enormous technical demands that can only be met by using chemicals, UV filtration and other elaborate techniques. Using chemicals to purify water often turns out to be a dead end – it is expensive in the long run and ecologically dubious for the water. It can also create a number of peripheral problems, such as restricted plant growth or offensive odours.

Water is much more readily accepted when it is clear. For this reason attention should be paid from the outset to the rubbish and pollutants that will come into contact with the water and to their sources. Some things will fall into the water naturally, some as a result of human intervention. Fallen

leaves or road dust, but also food for ducks and fish (this should not be underestimated as a problem), and remains of human food and packaging will likely end up in the water. Any open water is polluted by such materials, which are either dissolved in it, or remain undissolved. It is therefore very important to know about any sources of pollution at the planning stage, and to estimate the nature and scale of their possible effects on the water feature.

The choice of which water technology is ultimately installed is influenced by all these prior considerations and investigations of processes in the water system. Courageous decisions about ecologically sensible solutions take pressure off the environment and can set new standards that lead to genuine innovation. Learning from nature and using the insights gained for new concepts is also a relevant planning approach here.

General plan for
plant room and
circulation cistern

Plant room

Multilayer filter

Circulation cistern

Pump in pump well

Water drain

Filter manhole

Pumps on plinth

Pump in pump well

Construction elements

Water features cannot be built without technical equipment like reservoirs, pumps, filters and control devices. These are needed to purify the water, to store it and to control its circulation.

Storage and circulation cisterns: All water features with a circulating water system need a cistern or storage reservoir to ensure that there is always enough water available for them to run on. When small quantities of water are involved it is usually sufficient to install a cistern near the feature where the water can fall to by gravity. The cistern or reservoir has to be big enough for all the water to be stored after the feature has been switched off. The circulating volume consists of the amount of water circulating in all the pipes, channels and pools, and has to be specifically fixed for each feature.

It is not unusual for mistakes to be made when calculating for large volumes of water. The volume flowing out of a feature must be the same as the volume flowing in. The smaller and narrower the outlet, the more the water will back up. This variation in water level has thus to be assessed as a volume and the water level has to be able to rise accordingly.

Water from the cistern is either brought by suction to the pumps in the plant room or pumped directly back into the circulation system by a submerged pump in the cistern. When features have a low-lying body of water like a pool or pond, these can be used as a reservoir and thus a separate cistern is not needed. Additional water is then fed directly into the body of water. It is important that every storage reservoir or cistern is provided with an overflow as well as a drainage outlet so that it can be emptied and cleaned at regular intervals.

Pumps: It is seldom that a water feature can be set to run on a natural slope. Normally the water has to be circulated artificially with pumps. As a rule these are modern rotary pumps that are set up in either a wet or a dry state. Dirty-water pumps are recommended if high dirt levels are anticipated.

Our experience is that it makes sense to run small fountains and watercourses with a circulation volume of up to 300 l/min with submerged pumps. But not all makes are entirely suitable for this. Submerged pumps are usually more reasonably priced than dry-installed pumps, as they do not need their own control room and can be placed directly in the reservoir. They are more expensive to maintain than dry-installed pumps. Submerged pumps must always be set up so that they are sufficiently above the bottom of the feature to avoid clogging with mud.

Dry-installed pumps are recommended when several pumps are required or they have to be set up in sequence. They are more accessible and thus easier to maintain, but they need adequate installation space. The best place is in a building near to the water feature or a readily accessible service shaft. Here it is essential to build in a bottom outlet to the channel and also ventilation where necessary. Dry-installed pumps do not run silently even when fitted with vibration dampers; for this reason they should be sited so that sound

Bank zone　　　Drainage manhole　　　　　　　　　　　　　　　　Circulation cistern

Infiltration gravel

Return duct

Pressure
feeder pipe

Pump

Section through
pond drainage and
storage cistern

emissions are kept reduced to a minimum.

The size of the pumps should not be decided until the volume of circulating water has been fixed. The manufacturer's technical specifications can be used as a guide. In the case of prototype features with special flow effects the size of the pumps should not be fixed without testing in a full-scale model. A certain circulation reserve should always be built in when choosing the size of the pumps so that the water quantities can be regulated if necessary. Maximum performance in relation to energy used can be achieved by pumps with automatic revolution speed controls, but this elaborate technology does not come cheap.

Filters: In nature water is continuously filtered in a number of ways such as percolating through vegetated soil, or by water animals. Filtering of this kind is also needed in artificial waters, especially when a lot of foreign bodies may find their way into it. Man contributes to this as well as nature – for example with plastic bags, cola cans, food scraps, plastic straws, cigarette ends and so on.

The first planning aim should always be to avoid dirt and rubbish entering the water in the first place. Where this is not possible the substances, which are often floating and do not dissolve, must be filtered out as soon after they enter the water as possible. In the case of circulation features this is done by coarse pre-filters like skimmers, rakes of perforated metal sheeting that are usually built into the feedback to the cistern. Various grades, from coarse to fine filtering, should be chosen, according to the amount of dirt involved. A filter with a mesh larger than 10 millimetres is considered coarse in this context. These should be simple and quick to handle, as otherwise manual cleaning tends to be carried out rarely or not at all. Stainless steel has proved its worth as a construction material for these pre-filters.

It makes sense to use automatic filter systems as well as pre-filters in more complex features; as a rule they are installed on the delivery side of the pump. These filters, including fast sand filters and micro-sieves, are outstandingly well suited for removing fine particles like weeds or floating matter from the circulating water. Maintenance requirements are low, as these filters can be set to clean themselves automatically from time to time. Automatic filters should be fitted in the bypass

Section through
equipment room

Operational diagram
for circulation technology

Return pipes

Circulation cistern

Supply pipes

Micro-sieve

Multilayer filter

Collection pool

Pumps

Pump well

to the circulation tank, and should ideally be able to filter about 50 % of the total water in circulation.

We have found that naturally developed sand or bottom filters, here called purification biotopes, are suitable for many water features. They are particularly appropriate for features and systems that allow the watercourse to develop naturally to a certain extent, and that have sufficient space available. They have various advantages; they form second-hand biotopes, do not need any additional energy and are not expensive to maintain. As with any other planting, dead vegetable matter and foreign bodies have to be removed from time to time. The winter months are most suitable for this.

Regulation and monitoring: Every water system needs regulation. This ensures that the various input points are provided with the appropriate quantities of water at the required time. When the water level drops in the cistern or the body of water an electrical or mechanical sensor should monitor the water level and ensure that the necessary extra water is fed in. The control boxes and all the meters should always be installed above maximum water level in a separate shaft or in the cellars of an adjacent building. In the case of larger and more complex features there will be meters for certain parameters like pH value, temperature, oxygen content or nutrient levels in the water, working continuously or sporadically. These values then form a basis for precise analysis of the water. Some clients like the feature to be monitored so that they can optimize development and also the maintenance of the system and the related costs on the basis of suggestions from experts.

Section through
purification biotope

Purification biotope

Bank zone

Round gravel 4/8 mm

Irrigation hose

Plant substrate

Railway ballast 56/63 mm

Sealing structure

Drainage layer with pipe

Open water

Mirror

Sound and light
column

Glass column

90

500

Metal plinth

70

Loud speakers

240

Light/sound technology: Lighting and sound effects are becoming increasingly desired by the client. They enhance the effects of a water feature and give the experience a new dimension, especially in the evening and at night. It is essential to investigate the existing light and sound situation of the site, in order to assess their influence.

In many cases no elaborate electronic systems are needed. The interaction of air and water alone produces all sorts of sound patterns that can be used to good effect within a spatial concept. The rush of water has other qualities to offer than traffic noise, for example, and can be used deliberately to dampen or mask unpleasant noises and at the same time offers the opportunity to create a special atmosphere in a particular place.

Water cannot be lit like other objects. If artificial light is used, care has to be taken that the water itself can direct the light, and here reflected light is crucial. Before choosing a light source it is essential to conduct experiments to establish the desired effect of light on the water.

This effect is crucially dependent on the reflection of light from the surface of the water; it is only this that makes the water visible. Skilful light installation can also achieve these effects in twilight and at night.

If lighting is to be effective it is essential that the source points are positioned correctly. Lighting the water directly is not recommended, as the light would be reflected only at certain points. It is better to draw the observer's attention to adjacent objects. They will be reflected from the surface and will produce the fluctuating images associated with water

with even a very little movement.

Lighting devices should be chosen in such a way that insects are not attracted in greater numbers, and to avoid increased weed growth in the water. This means that halogen lamps with a large UV output are not suitable; metal vapour lamps tend to be most used today.

Fibre-optic technology is particularly suitable for underwater lighting. The key feature here is that the light source can be placed at a safe distance from the body of water, and the fibre technology can take the light wherever it is wanted.

Drainage gully

Stone edge on mortar bed

Impermeable liner

Natural stone slabs on chippings

Tunnel roof

Fixing anchor

Section through piazza ditch to tunnel roof

Construction technology

Technical aspects of construction are of crucial importance for interesting water features with high design values. Interest is focused on the following four areas: sealing, foundations, materials and connections.

Sealing: Natural seals like clay can rarely be used in built water features. There are many sealing processes that are quite close to nature, but a certain diffusion loss has to be anticipated with all of them. Such processes are suitable only when continuous supply and constant water level are guaranteed.

When choosing a sealant the necessities arising from the specific situation have to be set off against the technical and financial input involved. The following criteria should be considered: the qualities of the building land, the geometry and surface of the feature, the desired water quality, the planned building phases and the cost.

Water features that are supplied and drained naturally make fewer demands in terms of sealing than those that rely on an artificial supply of drinking water or rainwater. However, minimal water loss should be a prime consideration even for small water features, for ecological and financial reasons.

Plastic sheeting is very adaptable as a sealing material, and is well suited to features with complex contours and very diverse geometry. But natural forms can be constructed with it as well. Many water features have to take differing settling rates into account. Flexible sheeting is suitable here, as it is relatively easy to install on the spot, almost regardless of the weather. A whole variety of materials are available; of course their environmental friendliness must be given higher priority than technical suitability and economic viability.

If the substructure is something stable like concrete, for instance, a non-shrink grouting compound can also be used as a seal. It bonds firmly with the base and is simple to apply even if the geometry is complex. Coverings like natural stone slabs can be fitted directly to the rigid seal. This is also appropriate for fixed materials like concrete and steel, but does not work with flexible connections or expansion joints; other sealing processes have to be used here.

Water features in the shape of simple and rigid structures can be built in non-permeable concrete. However, these are appropriate only when the subsoil is stable, certain dimensions are not exceeded and walls of an adequate thickness can be built. The statics of water-proof concrete make it particularly suitable as a base for large prefabricated sections.

Pavement gutter Concrete elements Foundation Slab Ballast support layer

Section through watercourse

Foundations: Semi-natural lakes and ponds do not need rigid foundations. But fountains, pools and other built water features are particularly sensitive to subsoil settling, which can lead to cracks and leaks. What is usually needed here is foundations that can have a frost-free base and that are designed to meet the structural loading. The dimensions and thickness of the foundations are based on the weight, geometry, size and tolerance limit of the surface building.

Choice of materials: Unlike other structures, built water-features have surfaces that are always wet. For this reason it is important to use materials that are structurally stable and also frostproof in colder regions. Another important factor is that chemical and physical reactions of materials can be different and more aggressive in contact with water than in air, and vary with the characteristics of the water (pH value, temperature etc.). Building materials must be chosen to withstand such processes in the long term. Water quality must also be taken into account when choosing materials, as substances dissolved out of mortar or concrete can have a lasting deleterious effect on water chemistry.

In the case of earth and mineral substrates, chemical stability and the purity of the material are important factors. Organic components should be avoided wherever possible, as they raise nutrient levels and thus promote the growth of algae.

The colour of these materials is a key influence on the visual impact of the water; here dark shades are generally better for reflections on the surface of the water whereas-

lighter shades are suitable for showing reflections on the bottom. However, it is not so important to design the surface of these coverings elaborately, as the effect they make will be considerably reduced by the natural surface growth that occurs in any water. This growth can only be avoided by mechanical cleaning or the use of chemicals.

Water features in which people are intended to walk should have non-slip surfaces to minimize the risk of falling. Sharp-edged installations should also be avoided as they increase the risk of injury.

Section through concrete element run and water-course

Concrete support structure
Fan jet 6/60 mm
Neoprene
Water borderstone
Mortar filling 45 mm
Protective layer 3 mm
Waterproof layer 2,5 mm
Fleece 500 g/m2
Control sensor

Fitting the waterproof
layer with adhesive strip

Interfaces: Natural watercourses are always in a state of dynamic interchange with their surroundings, losing water through outflow, evaporation and infiltration. Artificial water features would quickly lose their water to the surrounding area. To prevent this, the interface is particularly important, as well as sealing.

The interface between inflow, outflow, pipes and walls always presents a potential danger in terms of leaks; this is where most problems occur in practice. Different construction methods are required according to the nature of the seal. Connections through sheeting require fundamentally different flange constructions from those used for pierced concrete, for instance. For this reason precise and early planning is needed here, and particularly careful attention must always be paid to the construction and detailing of these points. Some specialist manufacturers offer prefabricated pipe ducting for seals of all kinds.

Detail of pipework

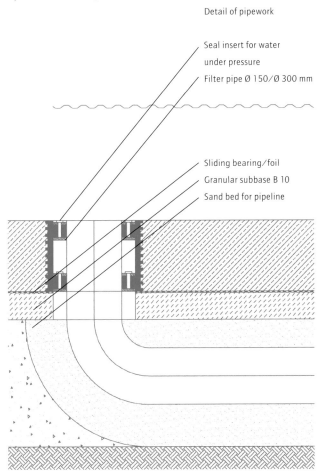

Seal insert for water
under pressure
Filter pipe Ø 150/Ø 300 mm

Sliding bearing/foil
Granular subbase B 10
Sand bed for pipeline

— Natural granite slab
— Railway ballast
— Gravel 5/25 mm
— Substrate
— Protective layer 3 mm
— Waterproof layer 2,5 mm
— Fleece 500 g/m²
— Control sensor

Running and maintenance

People who own and run a water feature will soon become disillusioned with it if it costs more than a modest amount to maintain. Planning should thus aim to avoid high maintenance and running expenses. A number of very creatively successful water features have been closed because of technical problems, the need for frequent repair work and unduly high running costs.

Traditionally fountains and other running water features are closed in winter. But it is possible to run them all the year round if appropriate preventive measures are taken, like frost-proof water storage facilities and a heated water supply.

A thorough planning approach will pay particular attention to the later running of the water feature. More or less elaborate solutions will be selected according to location. The centre of a large city imposes different requirements and thus needs different creative and technical concepts from those appropriate to small towns or villages. An intensively used feature should therefore not just be well designed, but above all well looked after as well. Here we must not fail to recognize that ornately designed components will always be more likely to be damaged than robust elements. The finished product should be selected to match the location in a way that does not encourage increasing tendencies to vandalism.

In the long run, water features work best if they are as clearly and simply planned as possible. Logical arrangements and structures for the various units and sections make them easier to service. To avoid periods of malfunction, or to keep them as short as possible, it makes sense for large water features to use parts from the same manufacturer. This makes it easy to replace components and also simplifies storage.

All electrical devices in the wet area inside and outside the water feature must be appropriately protected and fused to meet safety standards. This includes current failure protection circuits, damp and wet fittings, low voltage installations and appropriate earthing for all live electrical parts.

Staff often find a service manual helpful. This should contain lists of all the maintenance work needed, instructions on how to behave in case of emergency, and guidelines for running the system in winter.

Technical data

Page 12

Tanner Springs Park,
Portland, Oregon, USA
Client: City of Portland
Landscape design:
Atelier Dreiseitl
Art wall: Herbert Dreiseitl
Local landscape architects:
GreenWorks, PC
Supervision: GreenWorks,
PC/Atelier Dreiseitl
Planning and design:
2002–2004
Construction: 2004–2005

Size: 4,800 m²
Circulation rate: 3 l/s
Maximum turnover: 20 h
Water treatment: Cleansing
biotope 444 m²
Length of art wall: 50 m
Steel rails: 360 pieces
Water surface: 520 m²
Total water volume: 238 m²

Page 18

Town square Hattersheim
Client: Stadt Hattersheim
Water design:
Herbert Dreiseitl
Landscape design:
Atelier Dreiseitl
Architect: Büro Walter,
Wiesbaden
Stone masonry:
Fa. Hettinger
Planning and design:
1988–1992
Construction: 1989–1993

Size: 4,600 m²
Watercourse length: 120 m
Water surface:
2,000 m² pond
Total water volume:
2,000 m³
Flow rate: 450 l/min
Maximum water depth:
250 cm
Minimum water depth: 5 cm
Water treatment:
Purification biotope
Pump power: 1.2 kW

Page 22

Musical fountain L'Aubier
near Neuchâtel, Switzerland
Client: L'Aubier, Montezillon
Design: Herbert Dreiseitl
**Details and Landscape
design:** Atelier Dreiseitl
Architect: Kurt Hofmann
Metalworks: Metallatelier
David Fuchs
Planning and design: 1990
Construction: 1991–1992

Size: Two storey object,
height 6 m
System:
Perforated collection piping
Length: 30 m watercourse
through the building
Flow rate: 2 l/min
Water treatment: Macro-
and micro-filtering systems

Page 24

Herne-Sodingen Academy
Client: EMC Entwicklungs-
gesellschaft Mont Cenis
Water design:
Atelier Dreiseitl
Architects:
Jourda Architects,
HHS Planer und Architekten
Project management:
dmp GmbH
Planning and design:
1998–1999
Construction: 1999

Watercourse length: 180 m
Water basin: 720 m²
Flow rate:
250 l/min watercourse
3,200 l/min water basin
Water depth:
30 cm watercourse
40 cm water basin
Cistern volume:
10 m³ watercourse
12 m³ water basin
Water treatment:
Multi-layered filter system
Pump power:
1 kW watercourse
3 kW water basin

Page 30

Watercourse and water wall
Gummersbach
Client:
Stadt Gummersbach
Sparkasse Gummersbach
Water design:
Herbert Dreiseitl
Landscape design:
Atelier Dreiseitl
Urban design:
Gruppe Hardtberg
Architect: Axel von Reden
Contractors:
Glasgestaltung Dierig
Metallatelier Fuchs
Planning and design:
1997–1999
Construction: 1998–1999

Length: 200 m
Circulation rate: 500 l/min
Water storage: 30 m³
Water treatment:
Sand filter
Pump power: 2.5 kW

Page 36

Vivaldi Amsterdam,
The Netherlands
Client: ING Real Estate
**Landscape architect
and water design:**
Atelier Dreiseitl
Architect: Norman Foster
and Partners
Planning and design:
2003–2005
Construction: 2005–2007

Site area: 1,760 m²
Water surface: 1,230 m²
Annual rainfall: 819 mm
Rainfall intensity:
For overflow 300 l/s/ha
Drainage method:
Green roof (extensive,
intensive), fluctuating water
level of 5 cm, 100 m² cistern,
overflow to the Spoorslag-
sloot Canal
Circulation rate: 11 l/s
Water treatment:
Cleansing biotope cleansing
2.5 l/s, skimmer, coarse filter
Stormwater event:
Less than 1 year

Page 38

Residential development
'Im Park', Bern-Ittigen,
Switzerland
Client: Berner Lebens-
versicherungs-Gesellschaft
Water design:
Herbert Dreiseitl
Landscape design:
Atelier Dreiseitl
Architect: René Burkhalter
AG, Architectur Design
Planning and design:
1988–1989
Construction: 1989–1990

Size: 6,000 m²
Watercourse length: 60 m
Water surface: 200 m²
Total water volume: 15 m³
Flow rate: 500 l/min
Maximum water depth:
40 cm
Cistern volume: 10 m³
Water treatment:
Technical filter
Pump power: 4 kW
Total area: 800 m² roof
Residents: 700
Impermeable surface: 60 %
Annual rainfall: 900 mm
Drainage method: Open
surface drains, retention
pond

Page 46

Potsdamer Platz, Berlin
Client: Stadt Berlin/
Debis Immobilien
Water design:
Atelier Dreiseitl
Architects: Renzo Piano,
Christoph Kohlbecker
Project management:
Atelier Dreiseitl + Peter
Hausdorf
Planning and design:
1994–1998
Construction: 1997–1998

Water surface: approx.
12,000 m²
Shoreline and edges:
1,700 m
Overflow edge: 44 m
Total water volume:
approx. 12,000 m³
Flow rate: 500 m³/h
Turnover: 3 days
Minimum water depth:
30 cm
Maximum water depth:
185 cm
Cistern volume: 2,000 m³
Water treatment:
Purification biotope
1,900 m² surface area
Pump power: 100 kW
Connected roof area:
Paved roof 32,000 m²
Green roof 12,000 m²
Annual rainfall: 530 mm
Drainage method:
Evaporation approx.
11,570 m³/ annum,
toilet flushing approx.
10,800 m³/ annum,
irrigation approx.
1,114 m³/ annum,
overflow in Landwehrkanal
max. 3 l/s/ha
**Emergency overflow in
canal:** 0,2 %
Retention volume: Water
basin 3,100 m³

Page 53

Prisma Nuremberg
Client: Karlsruher Lebens-
versicherung AG
Water design, glass design:
Herbert Dreiseitl
Landscape design:
Atelier Dreiseitl
Architect: Joachim Eble
Architektur
Climate simulation:
Dr. Wilhelm Stahl
Metalworks:
Metallatelier Fuchs
Glassworks: Glasgestaltung
Dierig
Planning and design:
1992–1994
Construction: 1993–1997

Size: Glass house volume
15,000 m³, glass house
area 1,400 m², external
planting 870 m²
Length: 110 m watercourse
Water surface: 240 m²
Total water volume: 60 m³
Flow rate: 1,200 l/min
Maximum water depth:
35 cm
Minimum water depth: 5 cm
Cistern volume:
240 m³ rainwater storage
Water treatment:
190 m² planters,
filters, sedimentation in
cistern, purification biotope
50 m² surface area
Pump power:
14 kW (2 x 5.5/1 x 3)
Site area: 6,000 m²
catchment area
Residents: 160
Impermeable surface:
100 %
Annual rainfall: 675 mm
Rainfall intensity: $r_{15(1)}$
117.8 l/s/ha

Drainage method:
Evaporation, infiltration
underneath building, re-use
(irrigation)
**Soil permeability
factor:** 1×10^{-4} m/s sand
subsoil, distance to groundwater table $\geq$13 m
**Infiltration and
retention area:**
474 m² under underground
parking,
105 m² pond
Stormwater event:
10 years

Page 59	**Page 60**	**Page 62**	**Page 66**	**Page 69**

Page 59

Art and rainwater object
Owingen
Client: Gemeinde Owingen
Water design:
Herbert Dreiseitl
Water planning:
Atelier Dreiseitl
Architect: Huber & Böhler
Metalworks:
Metallatelier Fuchs
Planning and design: 1998
Construction: 1998

Roof area: 1,200 m^2,
with 40 % green roof
Annual rainfall: 780 mm
Rainfall intensity: r$_{15(1)}$
142 l/s/ha)
Drainage method: Constructed infiltration swales
Soil permeability factor:
≤1 x 10^{-5} m/s
Infiltration and retention
area: 50 m^2
Stormwater event: 2 years

Page 60

Redesign Queens Botanical
Garden, New York, USA
Client: City of New York and
Queens Botanical Garden
Landscape design:
Atelier Dreiseitl, Conservation Design Forum
Architect: BKSK, New York
Planning and design:
2000–2004
Construction: 2004–2006

Site area: 15,800 m^2
Green roof: 490 m^2
Constructed wetland
(Greywater system): 180 m^2
Watercourse length: 200 m
Annual rainfall: 1,070 mm
Rainfall intensity:
6 min. rainfall;
160 mm/h = 10 year storm
event
Drainage method:
Drainage swale and ditch,
infiltration swale
Release rate: 960 l/s
(total area)
Water treatment:
Cleansing biotope
105 m^2
Soil permeability factor:
10^{-7} m/s
Infiltration and retention
area: 3,720 m^2
Stormwater event: 10 years

Page 62

Solar City Linz, Austria
Client: Stadt Linz
Water design:
Herbert Dreiseitl
Landscape design:
Atelier Dreiseitl
Architects: READ-Gruppe
Competition: 1997
Planning and design:
1998–2001
Construction: 1999–2005

Size: 60 ha
Settlement area: 32 ha
Residents: 4,500
Impermeable surface: 40 %
Water surface: Extension
of Weikerlsee approx.
29,000 m^2
Water playgrounds:
1,000 m^2
Total water volume:
90,000 m^3
Maximum water depth:
400 cm
Water treatment:
Purification biotope
200 m^2 surface area
Annual rainfall: 800 mm
Rainfall intensity: r$_{15(1)}$
125 l/s/ha
Drainage method:
Drainage and infiltration
(emergency overflow >10 a
into Aumühlbach and woodland area along the Traun)
Soil permeability factor:
Swales 10^{-4}, trenches 10^{-2}
Infiltration and retention
area: 9,000 m^2
Stormwater event: 10 years

Page 66

Bear enclosure at Zoo Zurich,
Switzerland
Client: Zoo Zurich
Planning of water system:
Atelier Dreiseitl
Landscape design:
Büro Walter Vetsch
Planning and design:
1993–1995
Construction: 1995–1997

Size: 4,500 m^2
Length: 45 m
Water surface: 200 m^2
Total water volume: 300 m^3
Flow rate: 2,000 l/min
Maximum turnover rate:
2.5 hrs.
Maximum water depth:
150 cm
Cistern volume: 15 m^3
Water treatment:
Purification biotope
105 m^2 surface area
Pump power: 7 kW

Page 69

Open space and water
design, Fornebu, Oslo,
Norway
Client: National Construction
Department (Staatsbygg)
Landscape design:
Bjørbekk & Lindheim
Water design:
Herbert Dreiseitl/Atelier
Dreiseitl
Planning and design:
2004–2005
Construction: 2006–2007

Site area: 46.75 ha
(= 467,500 m^2)
Water surface:
Central Lake 6,000 m^2,
Water channel 1,460 m^2
Total water volume:
Central Lake 9,000 m^2
Watercourse length: 460m
Annual rainfall: 711 mm
Rainfall intensity: r$_{15(1)}$
85 l/s/ha
Drainage method:
Drainage swale and ditch,
retention swale, retention
with fluctuating lake water-
level (20 cm), retention and
infiltration in 'Frog Wetland',
street run-off treatment with
sand filter, overflow into
natural wetland

Water technique for lake
and channel:
Circulation rate: 50 l/s
Release rate: 120-150 l/s
Water treatment:
Cleansing biotope 1,000 m^2,
skimmer (2 pieces), micro-
screen (20 micrometres/6 m^2)
groundwater recharge (1 l/s)
Soil permeability factor:
10^{-5} m/s
Infiltration and retention
area 'Frog Wetland': 3,600 m^2
Stormwater event: 2 years

Page 70

Sonnenhausen Estate, Glonn
Client: K. L. Schweisfurth
Stiftung, Hermannsdorfer
Landwerkstätten
Water design:
Herbert Dreiseitl
Landscape design:
Atelier Dreiseitl
Planning and design:
1987–1988
Construction: 1989

Size: 4,000 m² roof area,
18,000 m² open space
Site area: 22,000 m²
Length: 150 m
Water surface: 2,000 m²
Total water volume:
2,000 m³
Flow rate: 100 l/min
Maximum water depth:
130 cm
Minimum water depth:
20 cm
Water treatment:
Purification biotope
surface area 200 m²
Pump power: 0.75 kW
Residents: 40
Impermeable surface: 30 %
Annual rainfall: 850 mm
Drainage method: Surface
drains, retention pond
Soil permeability factor:
1 x 10⁻⁶ m/s
**Infiltration and retention
area:** 200 m²

Page 72

Arkadien Asperg
Client: Firma Strenger Bauen
und Wohnen
**Landscape design and water
design:** Atelier Dreiseitl
Architect:
Joachim Eble Architektur
Planning and design:
1999–2000
Construction: 2001–2003

Site area: 15,000 m²
Watercourse length: 100 m
Water surface: 300 m²
Total water volume: 30 m²
Flow rate: 400 l/min
Maximum water depth:
40 cm
Minimum water depth:
20 cm
Cistern volume:
Retention cistern
60 m², circulation cistern
15 m²
approx. 15 individual cisterns
of 3 m² in size
Annual rainfall: 750 mm
Rainfall intensity: $r_{15(1)}$
3.5 l/s/ha
Drainage method:
Drainage in open swale
and watercourse, storage for
toilet use, irrigation of green-
space and watercourse refill
Water treatment:
Division of total runoff,
coarse filter for cistern,
fine filter for toilet water
Pump power: 1.5 kW
Residents: 200
Impermeable surface: 70 %
Stormwater event: 5 years

Page 75

Garden Festival
Chaumont–sur-Loire, France
Client: Conservatoire Inter-
national des Parcs et Jardins
et du Paysage
Water design:
Herbert Dreiseitl
Planning and design:
2003–2004
Construction: 2004

Site area: 250 m²
Water surface:
180 m² ('Solid and Liquid')

Page 77

Coffee Creek Estate,
Indiana, USA
Client: Lake Erie Land
Water design:
Atelier Dreiseitl/
Conservation Design Forum
Landscape design:
Conservation Design Forum
Architect:
William McDonough +
Partners
Contractor:
Lakeshore Landscape/
Gough Construction
Planning and design:
1995–1999
Construction: 1998–2000

Size: 260 ha
Site area: 2,000 m² designed
watercourse
Watercourse length: 60 m
Width watercourse:
2–3.5 m
Flow rate: 3,000 l/min

Page 82

EXPO 2000 Hannover
Kronsberg
Client: Stadt Hannover,
Stadtentwässerung
**Water and landscape
design:** Atelier Dreiseitl
General drainage concept:
ARGE
Dreiseitl/ITWH/IFS
Planning and design:
1994–1999
Construction: 1999–2000

Cistern volume: 33 m³
Water treatment:
Purification biotope
400 m² surface area
Pump power: Solar pumps
with ca 1.5 kW each
Site area: 130 ha
Residents: 15,000
Impermeable surface: 80 %
Annual rainfall: 750 mm
Rainfall intensity: $r_{15(1)}$
100 l/s/ha
Drainage method:
Constructed swales,
retention basins, overflow
into Rohrgraben
Soil permeability factor:
$\leq 1 \times 10^{-6}$ m/s
**Infiltration and retention
area:** 50,000 m²
Release rate: 3 l/s/ha
Stormwater event: 35 years

Page 86

Scharnhauser Park, Ostfildern
Client: Stadt Ostfildern
Rainwater management:
Atelier Dreiseitl
Urban Design:
Janson & Wolfrum
Street planning: IB Gmelin
Planning and design:
1995–1999
Construction: 1996–2003

Site area: 140 ha
Settlement area: 70 ha
Residents: 9,000
Impermeable surface: 60 %
Annual rainfall: 700 mm
Rainfall intensity: $r_{15(1)}$
125 l/s/ha
Drainage method:
Constructed swales and
trenches, retention basins,
drainage to Höfelbach and
Krähenbach and further into
Körsch river
Soil permeability factor:
1×10^{-8} m/s
**Infiltration and retention
capacity:** 21,000 m³ swales,
16,000 m³ trenches
Release rate: 3 l/s/ha
Stormwater event: 5 years

Page 91

Toppilansaari, Oulu, Finland
Client: City of Oulu
Landscape design:
Atelier Dreiseitl
Water art features:
Herbert Dreiseitl
Architect:
Planning Department,
City of Oulu
Planning and design:
2003–2004
Construction: 2004–2005

Total area: 75,000 m²
Residents: 3,000
Impermeable area: 33 %
Discharge in stream:
Existing wetland/ocean
Annual rainfall:
460 mm (half snow)
Rainfall intensity: $r_{15(1)}$
5 year storm event, 180 min.,
32 l/s/ha
Drainage method:
Drainage swale and ditch,
infiltration swale
Soil permeability factor:
10^{-5} m/s, infiltration velocity
of 0.5 l/s/100 m²
**Infiltration and retention
area:** 1,200 m² infiltration
area, 1,000 m² retention
area
Stormwater event: 5 years
Cleansing biotope area:
approx. 30 m²

Page 94

Sewage treatment plant
Client: Treuhandverein
Wörme: e.V.
Design: Atelier Dreiseitl
Planning and design: 1993
Construction: 1994

Size: 900 m²
Purification biotope:
600 m² surface area
Site area: 37 ha
Residents: 80
System capacity: 100 people

Page 98

Redesign of Volme river and
town hall
Client: Stadt Hagen
Water design:
Herbert Dreiseitl
Landscape design:
Atelier Dreiseitl
Architects: RKW Architects
Hydraulics: Thomas Nill
Planning bridge:
PASD Feldmeier & Wrede
Planning and design:
2000–2001
Construction: 2001–2004

Length: Volme 800 m
Width: Volme 25 m
Total water volume:
Mean rate = 5.67 m³/s
Maximum rate 100 = 249.70
m³/s
Embankment redesign:
12,000 m²

Page 102

City Hall, Chicago, USA
Client: City of Chicago
Landscape design:
Atelier Dreiseitl/
Conservation Design Forum
Architects:
William McDonargh &
Partners
Planning and design:
1999–2000
Construction: 2000–2001

Size:
Roof area ≈ 3,600 m²,
planted area: 2,200 m²

| Page 105 | Page 108 | Page 110 | Page 114 | Page 118 |

Page 105

Redesign Lanferbach,
Gelsenkirchen
Client:
Emschergenossenschaft
**Water and landscape
design:**
Atelier Dreiseitl
Planning and design:
1994–1998
Construction: 1999

Size: 32,000 m^2
Length: 800 m
Site area: 12 ha
Residents: 1,900
Annual rainfall:
775–800 mm
Rainfall intensity: $r_{15(1)}$
115 l/s/ha
Drainage method:
Constructed swales and
trenches, infiltration basins
Soil permeability factor:
1 x 10^{-5} m/s
**Infiltration and retention
area:** 4,000 m^2
Release rate:
Mean rate = 7.5 l/s
Maximum rate = 76.1 l/s

Page 108

Estate 'Hameau de la
Fontaine', Echallens,
Switzerland
Client: Theiler & Partner,
Murten
**Water and landscape
design:**
Atelier Dreiseitl
Architects: Theiler & Partner
Planning and design:
1981–1984
Construction: 1982–1986

Size: 50,000 m^2
Length: 80 m permanent
watercourses
Water surface: 350 m^2
Total water volume: 250 m^3
Flow rate: 300 l/min
Maximum water depth:
120 cm pond
Minimum water depth:
5 cm channel
Cistern volume: 5 m^3
Water treatment:
Purification biotope
100 m^2 surface area
Pump power: 0.75 kW
Roof area: 2,200 m^2
Residents: 250
Impermeable surface: 60 %
Annual rainfall: 850 mm
Drainage method:
Surface drains, retention
pond, drainage into stream

Page 110

Business park Krems-Ost,
Austria
Client:
Magistrat der Stadt Krems
Rainwater management:
Atelier Dreiseitl
Street planning:
IB Spindelberger
Planning and design:
1995–1996
Construction: 1996–1998

Site area: 330,000 m^2
**Impermeable surface in
business park:** 80 – 90 %
Annual rainfall: 800 mm
Rainfall intensity: $r_{15(1)}$
83 l/s/ha
Drainage method:
Infiltration swales and basins
**Soil permeability
factor:** 1 x 10^{-3} m/s
**Infiltration and retention
area:** 3,280 m^2
Stormwater event: 5 years

Page 114

BUGA 97 Phenomena in
cooling tower
Client: Bundesgarten-
schau 97 GmbH
Artistic concept:
Herbert Dreiseitl
Design: Atelier Dreiseitl
Architects:
PASD Feldmeier & Wrede
Structural engineers:
IPP Polonyi & Partner
Consultants: Institut für
Strömungswissenschaften,
FH Konstanz, Max Planck
Institut Göttingen
Planning and design:
1994–1996
Construction: 1997

Tower height: 28 m
Visitor platform: approx.
300 m^2
Flow rate:
200 m^3/hr. (maximum)
Pump power: 5 kW

Page 118

Hølaløkka-Alna, Oslo,
Norway
Client: Water department,
City of Oslo
Landscape design:
Atelier Dreiseitl,
13.3 Multiconsult
Water design:
Atelier Dreiseitl,
13.3 Multiconsult
Calculations: Interconsult
Planning and design:
2003–2004
Construction: 2004–2005

Site area: 30,000 m^2
Length: 500 m
Annual rainfall: 680 mm
Rainfall intensity: $r_{15(1)}$
3.5 l/s/ha
Drainage method:
Drainage swale and ditch,
infiltration swale
Release rate:
Phase 1 - 120-150 l/s
Phase 2 - 200-800 l/s
Water treatment:
Cleansing biotope, settling
pond
Soil permeability factor:
5 x 10^{-4} m/s
Stormwater event: Swale
capacity for 2 year event
Retention volume for 5 year
event
Cleansing biotope area:
700 m^2
Retention area: Stormwater
wetland 1,600 m^2
Swimming pond 3,000 m^2

Page 121	Page 124	Pagfe 126	Page 128	Page 134

Page 121

Landing pier Immenstaad
am Bodensee
Client: Gemeinde
Immenstaad
Water design:
Herbert Dreiseitl
Landscape design:
Wolfgang Holste
Planning and design: 1990
Construction: 1991

Flow rate: 600 l/min
System: Pumped lake water
Pump power: 0.9 kW

Page 124

Water concept and design
for research centre, London,
UK
Water concept:
Atelier Dreiseitl
Water design:
Herbert Dreiseitl/Atelier
Dreiseitl
Architect: Norman Foster
and Partners
Planning and design:
2000–2002
Construction: 2002–2004

Site area: Building area
30,000 m²
Site total 72,000 m²
Water surface:
Lake 16,200 m²/25,000 m³
Annual rainfall: 640 mm
Rainfall intensity: $r_{15(1)}$
3.5 l/s/ha
Water treatment:
Cleansing biotope, 2,100 m²
area
Soil permeability factor:
No infiltration
**Infiltration and retention
area:** Overflow into river
Bourne
Stormwater event: 30 years
Length of cascade: 170 m
Flow rate: 200 l/s (normal)
330 l/s (maximum)
Heat exchanges: 9 mW
Cooling towers: 3 mW

Pagfe 126

Center of Excellence
(Maybach), Sindelfingen
Client: DaimlerChrysler
**Landscape design and water
design:** Atelier Dreiseitl
Planning and design:
2001–2002
Construction: 2001–2002

Size: 5,000 m²
Water surface: 1,050 m²
Annual rainfall: 750 mm
Rainfall intensity: $r_{15(1)}$
3.5 l/s/ha
Circulation rate: 2000 l/min
Water treatment:
Cleansing biotope
Cistern volume: 40 m²
Total water volume:
430 m² (pond)
Pump power:
10 kW total
Cleansing biotope area:
150 m²
Water depth: 0.40 m (pond)

Page 128

Pearl of Hangzhou, China
Client: Shui On Properties
Water concept:
Atelier Dreiseitl
Water design:
Atelier Dreiseitl
Architect:
Wood + Zapata, Shanghai
Planning and design:
2002–2003

Site area: 16,500 m²
Water surface: 5,300 m²
Cooling cascade: 250 m²
Water features: 1,300 m²
Waterfront: 300 m
Cleansing biotope: 3,000 m²
Annual rainfall: 1,500 mm
Rainfall intensity: $r_{15(1)}$
3.5 l/s/ha

Page 134

EXPO 2000 Water-
traces Hann. Münden
Client: Stadt Hann. Münden
Water design: 'Szene'
Herbert Dreiseitl
Planning and design:
Atelier Dreiseitl
Planning of squares:
BSF, Ulrich Franke
Artists:
'Hoch' Diether Heisig,
Uli Westerfrölke (air)
'Serie Speier' Jens and Hans-
Werner Kalkmann
'Tief und Streuung' Wolfgang
Rossdeutscher
'Klang, Dramaturgie'
Andres Bosshard
**Water carpet and sound/
light steles (steel):**
Metallatelier Fuchs
Glass:
Glasgestaltung Dierig
Planning and design:
1997–1999
Construction: 1999–2000

Size 'Szene': approx. 1,100 m²
Water surface: 180 m²
Flow rate: 400 l/min
Water depth: 4 cm
Cistern volume: 35 m³
Water treatment:
Reversible automatic
sandfilter
Pump power: 10.5 kW total
Catchment area: Church,
townhall 2,000 m²
Lighting: 50 m fibre optics
cables

Page 139	Page 140	Page 145	Page 146	Page 151

Page 139

Interior courtyard Nicolaus-
Cusanus-Haus, Stuttgart
Client: Baugemeinschaft
Birkach GBR
Water design:
Herbert Dreiseitl
Landscape design:
Atelier Dreiseitl/
G. Bockemühl
Architects: Bockemühl,
Weller und Partner
Planning and design:
1987–1990
Construction: 1990–1991

Size: 800 m²
Water surface: 70 m²
Flow rate: 100 l/min
Water depth basin: 25 cm
Water treatment:
Self-regulating
macro-filter
Pump power: 0.55 kW

Page 140

Heiner-Metzger Plaza,
Neu-Ulm
Client: City of Neu-Ulm
Water design:
Herbert Dreiseitl/
Atelier Dreiseitl
Landscape design:
Atelier Dreiseitl
Planning and design:
2003–2004
Construction: 2004–2005

Size: 2,100 m²
Water surface: 240 m²
Annual rainfall: 750 mm
Rainfall intensity: $r_{15(1)}$
114 l/s/ha
Drainage method:
Sedimentation manhole
Ø1,200, infiltration trench,
emergency overflow to
MW-Canal
**Flow rate for hydraulic
calculations:**
Q30 (0.2) = 15 l/s
Water technique:
Circulation rate 42 l/s,
Circulation cistern 25 m²
Water treatment:
Coarse filter 3 mm, bromine
disinfection
Soil permeability factor:
1.3×10^{-4} m/s (backfill, sand)
**Infiltration and retention
area:** 60 m²/20 m² retention
volume
Stormwater event: 5 years

Page 145

DWR Amsterdam,
The Netherlands
Client: DWR Water Manage-
ment Department
Water design:
Atelier Dreiseitl
Architect:
Hermann Hertzberger
Planning and design:
2004
Construction: 2005

Site area: 1,880 m²
Water surface: 1,400 m²
Annual rainfall: 819 mm
Rainfall intensity:
For overflow
300 l/s/ha
Drainage method:
Retention in water basin
with fluctuating water-level
(0.30 m), overflow to the
River Amstel
Circulation rate: 4 l/s
Water treatment:
Skimmer, coarse filter,
cleansing biotope
Retention area: 1,400 m²
Stormwater event: 7 years

Page 146

Restoration of Emscher River
Client: Emschergenossen-
schaft (German Sewer
Management Association)
Landscape architect:
Atelier Dreiseitl
**Emscher Masterplan
consultants:** Landschaft,
Planen & Bauen, ASTOC
Architects & Planners
Planning and design:
2003–2010
Construction: 2007–2014

Emscher watershed area:
430 km²
Emscher length: 60,000 m
Area population:
approx. 2 million
Sewage canal length: 51 km
Construction budget:
4.4 billion EUR

Westfalen Stadium:
Disconnection area:
22,000 m²
Soil permeability factor:
10^{-7} m/s
**Infiltration and retention
area:** 2,700 m²
Storage volume: 300 m²
Reduced release rate:
720 l/s (or 20 l/s/ha)

Emscher-Info-Park:
Site area: 65,000 m²
Platform area: 10,000 m²
Sludge tower diameter:
10,000 m²

Page 151

Water playground LGS 92,
Pforzheim
Client: Stadt Pforzheim
Water design:
Herbert Dreiseitl
Landscape design:
Atelier Dreiseitl
Planning and design:
1988–1989
Construction: 1990–1991

Size: 4,000 m²
Water surface: 300 m²
System: 80 %
circulation with 20 % permanent introduction of fresh
water
Total water volume: 60 m³
Flow rate: 150–300 l/min,
circulation partially manual

The authors

Herbert Dreiseitl, born in 1955, is a sculptor, water artist and landscape architect. After his studies, he set up his office, Atelier Dreiseitl, in Überlingen on Lake Constance in 1980. He has realised numerous projects in the fields of stormwater management, water art and landscape architecture. He is active in lecturing worldwide and his work is widely published.

Prof. Wolfgang Geiger is one of the few experts in natural water management. He is head of the Department of Water Management at the Universität Gesamthochschule in Essen, Faculty of Building.

Dieter Grau, born in 1963, gardener and landscape architect, has been working for the Atelier Dreiseitl since 1994. In 1996 he became head of the Landscape Architecture Department. He is involved in planning projects around the world and lectures frequently.

Prof. Detlev Ipsen teaches in the Department of Planning Method and Empirical Planning Research at the Gesamthochschule in Kassel, faculty of Urban and Regional Sociology. Editor of the publication 'Wasserkultur – Beiträge zu einer nachhaltigen Stadtentwicklung', Berlin, 1998.

Stefan Leppert, born in 1959, bank employee, gardener, engineering diploma in landscape architecture, specialist editor for the magazine 'Garten + Landschaft' in Munich, owner of the 'phase_neun' editorial office in Münster since spring 2001.

Wolfram Schwenk is a hydrobiologist and leading member of the private Institute of Flow Sciences in Herrischried in the southern Black Forest. The institute is known for Theodor Schwenk's book 'Sensitive Chaos' and is devoted to water research.

Robert Woodward, born in 1923 in Australia, studied architecture and landscape architecture in Sydney, where he directs his own water design office.

Illustration credits

Andreas Arnold
Pages: 30je, 34d

BKSK Architects
Pages: 61a

Andreas Bockemühl
Pages: 66abc, 67, 94abcde, 96c, 121ab, 157bc, 158a

Andreas Böhmer
Pages: 136e

Maarten Claasen
Pages: 145cfilo

Conne van D'Grachten
Pages: 140bc, 141, 143

Conservation Design Forum
Pages: 76, 77bcd

Debis Immobilien
Pages: 163bc

Aurel Dörner
Pages: 140ef, 142am

Herbert Dreiseitl
Pages: 12beh, 13ad, 14hk, 16acd, 18aehk, 19, 20abde, 21a, 22adgj, 23ad, 24b, 26dg, 27, 28gbehk, 29, 30abhk, 31, 33abdeh, 34ab, 35, 38ab, 39, 41abcde, 46abcdefg, 47, 48ae, 50abcdfg, 51, 56e, 62ad, 63ad, 70abc, 71, 76, 77a, 82d, 83a, 84ab, 86a, 88abcdfgh, 89, 91l, 92abdeh, 93, 95, 96ab, 98ab, 102c, 105b, 108abcde, 109, 114abcde, 115, 120, 121c, 122abcde, 123a, 135, 136abc, 138, 139abcd, 140dgj, 142dghil, 146dgjm, 150a, 151abcdef, 154abc, 155abcde, 156abc, 157a, 158bc, 159bc, 160abcdef, 161abc, 162abcde, 163a, 164, 165

City of Chicago - Mark Farina
Pages: 102afj, 103a

Foster and Partners
Pages: 37

David Fuchs
Pages: 98h, 101f

Ulf Glänzer
Pages: 146f

Siegfried J. Gragnato
Pages: 52, 53a, 57, 72bdegj

Dieter Grau
Pages: 50e, 58, 59abcd, 73, 82abc, 83b, 86fi, 90ad, 91cfi, 100c, 104, 105acde, 106abcd, 107, 126cf, 127, 140am

Werner Hannappel
Pages: 116abcde

Hanuschke & Schneider
Pages: 134c, 137d

Gerhard Hauber
Pages: Cover, 64h, 65ad, 124afl, 125ad

Jan Hilbert
Pages: 60adg, 144, 145m

Thomas Hoffmann
Pages: 53b, 55a, 88e, 110abc, 111abc

Brant Kilber
Pages: 16k, 34a, 55b, 56abcd, 134abd, 159a

Büro Kohlbecker
Pages: 126ai

Henry Kunowski
Pages: 12ad, 14abdg, 16gj

Berner Leben
Pages: 38c, 40

Doug Macy
Pages: 14e, 15, 17

Multiconsult, Section 13.3
Pages: 118adg, 119ad

Entwicklungsgesellschaft Mont Cenis mbH
Pages: 25, 26a

Büro PASD
Pages: 99ad, 101a

StPL/Pertlwieser
Pages: 62c, 64f

Jens Pfisterer
Pages: 32

Hendrik Porst
Pages: 146i, 148acf

Dominik Rottweiler
Pages: 136d

Dietmar Schellinger
Pages: 72a

Katja Schlichting
Pages: 74, 75adcf

Büro Stöckl
Pages: 64e

3 D Visual
Pages: 48bc

Harald Wegener
Pages: 137a